Super Cheap Florence Travel Guide 2021

Our Mission	6
Redefining Super Cheap	10
Discover Florence	14
Some of Florence's Best Bargains	16
Planning your trip	22
Hack your Florence Accommodation	24
The best price performance location in Florence	31
Use our FREE	32
accommodation finder service	32
How to be a green tourist in Florence	34
Saving money on Florence Food	36
SNAPSHOT: How to enjoy a $1,000 trip to Florence for $172	38
Unique bargains I love in Florence	39
How to use this book	40
OUR SUPER CHEAP TIPS…	42
Cheapest route to Florence from America	42
Arriving	43
Getting around	44
Orientate yourself with this free tour	45
Consider the Firenzecard	47
Book this incredible secret tour	48

Visit these Amazing Museums for free	49
Il Duomo di Firenz	50
Go to the oldest art gallery in the world	52
Visit David at Accademia	53
Bargello Museum	54
Basilica di Santa Croce	55
Palazzo Pitti	56
People Watch in Florence's Squares	57
Go Church Hopping	58
Visit the Best Markets	59
Parks and Gardens	61
Go Thrift shopping	62
Take a stroll	63
Visit Ponte Vecchio	64
Take a day trip to Pisa	65
Escape the crowds	66
Nightlife	68
Don't leave Florence without seeing (even if only from outside)	69
Is the tap water drinkable?	74
How much can you save haggling here?	74
Food and drink hacks	75
Must-try Florence food	77

Cheap Eats	78
Need to Know before you go	82
Language	83
Getting Out of Florence cheaply	84
Avoid these tourist traps or scams	85
RECAP: How to have a $1,000 trip to Florence on a $172 budget	86
Fully costed Breakdown	88
Thank you for reading	96
Bonus Budget Travel Hacks	100
How to find the freedom to travel	102
HOW TO FIND CHEAP FLIGHTS	106
Frequent Flyer Memberships	110
Pack like a Pro	111
Checks to Avoid Fees	112
Relaxing at the airport	114
Money: How to make it, spend it and save it while travelling	116
How to earn money WHILE travelling	117
How to spend money	119
How to save money while travelling	122
Travel Apps That'll Make Budget Travel Easier	125
How NOT to be ripped off	126

Small tweaks on the road add up to big differences in your bank balance	129
Where and How to Make Friends	132
When unpleasantries come your way…	133
Your Car rental insurance is crazy expensive	136
The best Travel Gadgets	141
Hacks for Families	143
Safety	146
Hilarious Travel Stories	148
How I got hooked on budget travelling	151
A final word…	153
Our Writers	154
Copyright	158

Our Mission

Like Simon Sinek said, "People don't buy what you do; they buy why you do it". We believe strongly that travel can and is best enjoyed on a budget.

If 2020 taught us anything it's this: Travel is a gift we must cherish and enjoy responsibly. The word responsible often evokes ideas of lavish spending. We have uncovered how to responsibly enjoy Florence on a tight budget.

Taking a trip to Florence is not just an outer journey, it's an inner one. Budget travel brings us closer to locals, culture and authenticity; which in turn makes our inner journeys more peaceful.

Travelling is painted as an expensive hobby; Travel guides, Travel bloggers and influencers often show you overpriced accommodation, restaurants and big-ticket attractions because they make money from our 'we're on vacation' mentality which leads to reckless spending. Our mission is to teach you how to enjoy more for less and get the best value from every Euro you spend in Florence.

This guide focuses on the cheap or free in Florence, but there is little value in travelling to Florence and not experiencing all it has to offer. Where possible we've included cheap workarounds or listed the experience in the loved but costly section - if it is worth your time and money.

We work to dispel myths, save you tons of money, teach you the local tips and tricks and help you find experiences in Florence that will flash before your eyes when you come to take your last breath on this beautiful earth.

Who this book is for and why anyone can enjoy budget travel

I've been travelling full-time for 20 years. I don't have a job and I'm not in any debt, which prompts friends and family to ask 'How can you afford to travel?'. My response? 'My passion is finding travel bargains'. This doesn't mean I do any less or sleep in dirty hostels. Someone who spends A LOT on travel hasn't planned or wants to spend their money. I believe you can live the bougie life on a budget; that's what I've been doing for the past 20 years.

Together with thrifty locals I met along the way I have funnelled my passion for travel bargains into 300 travel guides. In this guide, we have formulated a system to pass on to you, so you too can juice everything from visiting Florence while spending the least possible money.

There is a big difference between being cheap and frugal. I like to spend money on beautiful experiences, but 20 years of travel has taught me I could have a 20 cent experience that will stir my soul more than a $100 one. Of course, there are times when the reverse is true, my point is, spending money on travel is the best investment you can make but it doesn't have to be at levels set by hotels and attractions with massive ad spends and influencers who are paid small fortunes to get you to buy into something that you could have for a fraction of the cost.

I love travelling because it forces me to be present-minded. I like to have the cold hard budget busting facts to hand (which is why we've included so many one page charts, which you can use as a quick reference), but otherwise, I want to shape my own experience - and I'm sure you do too.

We have designed these travel guides to give you a unique planning tool to experience an unforgettable trip without spending the ascribed tourist budget.

When it comes to FUN budget travel, it's all about what you know. You can have all the feels without most of the bills. A few days spent planning can save you thousands. Luckily, Super Cheap Insider Guides have done the planning for you, so you can distill the information in minutes not days, leaving you to focus on what matters: immersing yourself in the sights, sounds and smells of Florence, meeting awesome new people and most importantly, feeling relaxed and happy. My sincere hope is that our tips will bring you great joy at a fraction of the price you expected.

So, grab a cup of tea, put your feet up and relax; you're about to enter the world of enjoying Florence on the cheap. Oh and don't forget a biscuit. You need energy to plan a trip of a lifetime on a budget.

Super Cheap Florence is not for travellers with the following needs:

1. You require a book with detailed offline travel maps. Super Cheap Insider Guides are best used with Google Maps - download before you travel to make the most of your time and money.
2. You would like thousands of accommodation, food and attraction recommendations; by definition, cheapest is most often singular. We only include maximum value recommendations. We purposively leave out over-priced attractions when there is no workaround.
3. You would like detailed write-ups about hotels/Airbnbs/Restaurants. We are bargain hunters first and foremost. We dedicate our time to finding the best deals, not writing flowery language about their interiors. Plus things change. If I had a pound for every time I read a Lonely Planet description only to find the place totally different, I would be a rich man. Always look at online reviews for the latest up to date information.

If you want to save A LOT of money while comfortably enjoying an unforgettable trip to Florence, minus the marketing, hype, scams and tourist traps read on.

Redefining Super Cheap

The value you get out of Super Cheap Florence is not based on what you paid for it; its based on what you do with it. You can only do great things with it, if you believe saving money is worth your time. Charging things to your credit card and thinking 'oh I'll pay it off when I get back' is something you won't be tempted to do if you change your beliefs now. Think about what you associate with the word cheap, because you make your beliefs and your beliefs make you.

I grew up thinking you had to spend more than you could afford to have a good time travelling. Now I've visited 190 countries I know nothing is further from the truth. Before you embark upon reading our specific tips for Florence think about your associations with the word cheap.

Here are the dictionary definitions of cheap:

1. costing very little; relatively low in price; inexpensive:
a cheap dress.
2. costing little labor or trouble:
Words are cheap.
3. charging low prices:
a very cheap store.
4. **of little account; of small value; mean; shoddy:**
cheap conduct; cheap workmanship.
5. **embarrassed; sheepish:**
He felt cheap about his mistake.
6. **stingy; miserly:**
He's too cheap to buy his own brother a cup of coffee.

Three out of six definitions have extremely negative connotations. The 'super cheap' we're talking about in this book is not shoddy, embarrassed or stingy. We donate 10% of our book profits to charity (details of the charities we support are at the end of the book) so you've already donated to charity just by buying this book - how is that stingy?

We added the super to reinforce our message. Super's dictionary definition stands for 'a super quality'. Super Cheap stands for enjoying the best on the lowest budget. Question other peoples definitions of cheap so you're not blinded to possibilities, potential, and prosperity. Here are some new associations to consider forging:

Shoddy

Cheap stuff doesn't last is an adage marketing companies have drilled into consumers. However by asking vendors the right questions cheap doesn't mean something won't last, I had a $10 backpack last for 8 years and a $100 suitcase bust on the first journey. A   out of San Francisco University found that people who spent money on experiences rather than things were happier. Memories last forever, not things, even expensive things. And as we will show you during this guide you don't need to pay to create great memories.

Embarrassed

I have friends who routinely pay more to vendors because they think their money is putting food on this person's table. Paradoxically, Cuban doctors are driving taxi's because they earn more money; it's not always a good thing for the place you're visiting to pay more and can cause unwanted distortion in their culture - Airbnb pushing out renters is an obvious example. Think carefully about whether the extra money is helping people or incentivising greed.

Stingy

Cheap can be eco-friendly. Buying thrift clothes is cheap but you also help the Earth. Many travellers are often disillusioned by the reality of traveling experience since the places on our bucketlists are overcrowded. Cheap can take you away from the crowds. You can find balance and harmony being cheap. Remember,"A journey is best measured in friends, rather than miles." – Tim Cahill. And making friends is free!

A recent survey by Credit Karma found 50% of Millennials and Gen Z get into debt travelling. **Please don't allow credit card**

debt to be an unwanted souvenir you take home. As you will see from this book, there's so much you can enjoy in Florence for free and so many ways to save money! You just need to want to!

Discover Florence

In 1339 Florence became the first city in Europe. The city has hardly changed since the Renaissance, narrow streets evoke a thousand tales, and its food and wine burst with historic flavour. Florence is the capital of Italy's Tuscany region, home to delicious Chinati red wine and more masterpieces of art and architecture than arguably any other city on earth.

The historic centre of Florence was named a World Heritage Site by UNESCO in 1982. Built on the site of an Etruscan settlement. Between 1865 and 1870 Florence was made capital of the united kingdom of Italy. More importantly, gelato was invented here in 1565 by a Florentine architect, it is still an art form today. You can watch master gelato servers wrap ice-cream onto cones for hours (or that might just be me).

Leonardo Da Vinci was born in the lower valley of the Arno River in the territory of Florence as was Gucci and Cavalli, who, like many a smart Florentine lives in the nearby wine-rich hills.

Florence is divided into four quarters, named after the most important churches. Three of them are on the right-hand bank of the river Arno; Santa Maria Novella, San Giovanni and the quarter of Santa Croce. The only quarter south of the river is Santo Spirito.

Florence is cheaper than Rome or Venice and it serves as a great spot for exploring the Tuscan countryside. And has the added benefit of being a compact city that is a pleasure to walk. Every single street in the center is a piece of history to explore.

10 million tourists descend on Florence every year so like any city that caters to tourists, Florence or as the Italians call it Firenze, can be a budget-buster, but take heart. The trick to keeping your trip affordable is to get off the tourist track and find the local deals.

If you follow the advice in this guide you could definitely get away with spending about $40 per person including accommodation.

Some of Florence's Best Bargains

How to Cut Queues

Time is money. Save yours for a fee of €3 per ticket (€4 for the **Uffizi** and Galleria dell'Accademia), by pre-booking your visit to Uffizi, Galleria dell'Accademia, Palazzo Pitti, Museo del Bargello and the Cappelle Medicee online.

It's only really essential to pre-book for Uffizi and Accademia as queues can be up to four hours long!

Pre-book direct with each museum. Don't book with for-profit intermediaries such as Florence.net or Tickitaly.com, or over the phone. Reservations are €5 more.

Booking links:

Uffizi: https://www.uffizi.it/en
Galleria dell'Accademia: http://www.galleriaaccademiafirenze.beniculturali.it/
Palazzo Pitti: https://www.uffizi.it/palazzo-pitti
Museo del Bargello: http://www.bargellomusei.beniculturali.it/
Cappelle Medicee: http://www.bargellomusei.beniculturali.it/musei/2/medicee/

Enjoy the best Florentine sandwiches

The cheapest, tastiest lunches in town come in sandwich form. Florentines adore Semel, where you can pickup a generously stuffed panini for €3.50.

Address: Piazza Lorenzo Ghiberti, 44/r, 50122

Enjoy Tuscan lunch on the cheap

Il Contadino is a locally loved Trattoria where delicious Tuscan lunch including meaty classics like roast rabbit and oven-roasted pork shank are served until 3.30pm and costs just €9 for two-courses!

Address: Via Palazzuolo 69-71

Stay in a frescoed palazzo on the cheap

'Set in an elegant palace in central Florence, Hotel Scoti provides classic-style rooms with fan and private bathroom, only 500 m from the Uffizi Gallery and Florence Cathedral is a 5-minute walk away.' Hotel Scoti offers rooms from just €35 a night - you won't find a hostel for this price in the same locale!

COVID-19 Money-saving Opportunities

Not a single person, for one moment, wants to profit from a global pandemic. Phil (our main contributor) sadly lost his aunt in London to the virus. As a team, we know first-hand the emotional devastation the pandemic has wreaked. Of course, it has also had a huge financial impact on many of our readers. That's why we decided it would be remiss of us, as a budget travel guide company if we did not point out the money-saving opportunities in Florence that have arisen because of the pandemic. Many economists predict 'a V-Shaped' Post-Virus recovery, meaning a fast rebound but inevitably some people will still be adversely affected and as travellers, we can and should help them. Therefore we have only included opportunities which help locals. We will keep you updated on the rebound deals as the year progress's via our blog at supercheapinsiderguides.com. For now, here are a few things in Florence to look out for:

- Look out for amazing value lunch deals. 6 euro lunch menus are being used to entice locals back to restaurants.
- Use NEW Airbnbs. New Airbnb listings are up 15% globally, due to the need for people to make money. Almost all with the NEW badge offer a substantial discount to first-time renters. Before booking check the profile of the person offering the new listing. Never book NEW Airbnbs offered by a profile without reviews or that was started this year. These tend to be scams, but if you're careful you can find a great apartment in Florence for half the normal price.
- Consider visiting Sicily after Florence. The authorities there are offering to cover half the cost of your flight and 1/3 of your accommodation costs.
- Take advantage of Budget carrier deals. Most Airlines in Florence were grounded for March and April, which means they are offering extremely low-cost

deals to entice customers back on board. Sign up to the newsletters of these carriers for the latest deals: Jetstar, Scoot, Air Asia, Cebu Pacific, and Lion Air

Note, If social distancing rules remain in place it may be cheaper to travel overland by train or bus, where possible. Airlines will increase prices because they'll only be able to sell two-thirds of their seats, leaving the middle seat empty for mandatory de-densification.

Planning your trip

When to visit?

The first step in saving money on your Florence trip is timing. If you are not tied to school holidays, the best time to visit is during the shoulder-season months of April, May, September and October. Florence gets about the same number of visitors as Rome but it is a fraction of the size. That means you're going to have to deal with crowded streets, accommodation shortages, and huge lines for just about everything (try to book ahead whenever possible). Traveling during the off-season or shoulder (low) season costs considerably less than traveling during high season. You will pay 40– 80 percent less during these times than in peak season.

Where to stay

Florence is a small city and generally a safe place where street-smart rules apply. My only strong advice is to avoid wandering around the Santa Maria Novella area at night, it gets dodgy.

If you're only staying a few days stay near to the Duomo, Piazza della Signoria or the Piazza Santa Croce. The O ltrarno and the hills are stunning, but in terms of seeing the main sights staying in those areas will cost you more time and money.

If you're a digital nomad you'll find Fiesole is the best price-performance area for longer-term stays. It has incredible views and offers easy access to the city. The best place for digital nomads to find long terms leases at a good price is: https://www.immobiliare.it/affitto-appartamenti/firenze/

The cheapest place to stay

If you're travelling solo hostels are your best option, both for meeting people and saving pennies.

Hostel Santa Monica is right next to the main canal and no more than 20 minutes walk to any of the main must-sees. Lovely room, great kitchen & common room and nice bathrooms. Lockers for each person provided with a key and a key is needed to get in as well as security cameras. At $20 for a dorm bed, its the cheapest place to lay your head in the city. Book ahead.

Airbnbs will be cheaper if you're travelling in a group but expect to stay a 40 minute from the sights for a decent price.

Get a five-star hotel on a hostel budget

Booking.com drop prices for many under capacity five-star hotels in the hopes you will spend money at their restaurants/ mini-bars etc. This only works in low-season or when there aren't many visitors in town for whatever reason. Check on the day you want to stay and book. It's useful when you need some serious rest and relaxation but remember this only works here if you book the same day as your stay, and only for one night and only in the low-season in Florence.

Hack your Florence Accommodation

Your two biggest expenses when travelling to Florence are accommodation and food. This section is intended to help you cut these costs dramatically before and while you are in Florence.

Hostels are the cheapest accommodation in Florence but there are some creative workarounds to upgrade your stay on the cheap.

Use Time

There are two ways to use time. One is to book in advance. Three months will net you the best deal, especially if your visit coincides with an event. The other is to book on the day of your stay. This is a risky move, but if executed well, you can lay your head in a five-star hotel for a 2-star fee.

Before you travel to Florence, check for big events using a simple google search 'What's on in Florence', if you find no big events drawing travellers, risk showing up with no accommodation booked (If there are big events on, demand exceeds supply and you should avoid using this strategy). Start checking for discount rooms at 11 am using a private browser on booking.com.

Before I go into demand-based pricing, take a moment to think about your risk tolerance. By risk, I am not talking about personal safety. No amount of financial savings is worth risking that. What I am talking about is being inconvenienced. Do you deal well with last-minute changes? Can you roll with the punches or do you freak out if something changes? Everyone is different and knowing yourself is the best way to plan a great trip. If you are someone that likes to have everything pre-planned using demand-based pricing to get cheap accommodation will not work for you. Skip this section and go to blind-booking.

Demand-based pricing

Be they an Airbnb host or hotel manager; no one wants empty rooms. Most will do anything to make some revenue because they still have the same costs to cover whether the room is occupied or not. That's why you will find many hotels drastically slashing room rates for same-day bookings.

How to book five-star hotels for a two-star price

You will not be able to find these discounts when the demand exceeds the supply. So if you're visiting during the peak season, or during an event which has drawn many travellers again don't try this.

On the day of your stay, visit booking.com (which offers better discounts than Kayak and agoda.com). Hotel Tonight individually checks for any last-minute bookings, but they take a big chunk of the action, so the better deals come from booking.com. The best results come from booking between 2 pm and 4 pm when the risk of losing any revenue with no occupancy is most pronounced, so algorithms supporting hotels slash prices. This is when you can find rates that are not within the "lowest publicly visible" rate. To avoid losing customers to other websites, or cheapening the image of their hotel most will only offer the super cheap rates during a two hour window from 2 pm to 4 pm. Two guests will pay 10x difference in price but it's absolutely vital to the hotel that neither knows it.

Takeaway: To get the lowest price book on the day of stay between 2 pm and 4 pm and extend your search radius to include further afield hotels with good transport connections.

How to trick travel Algorithms to get the lowest hotel price

Do not believe anyone who says changing your IP address to get cheaper hotels or flights does NOT work. If you don't believe us, download a Tor Network and search for flights and hotels to one destination using your current IP and then the tor network (a tor browser hides your IP address from algorithms. It is commonly used by hackers). You will receive different prices.

The price you see is a decision made by an algorithm that adjusts prices using data points such as past bookings, remaining capacity, average demand and the probability of selling the room or flight later at a higher price. If booking.com knows you've searched for the area before it will keep the prices high. To circumvent this, you can either use a different IP address from a cafe or airport or data from an international sim. I use a sim from Three, which provides free data in many countries around the world. When you search from a new IP address, most of the time, and particularly near booking you will get a lower price. Sometimes if your sim comes from a 'rich' country, say the UK or USA, you will see higher rates as the algorithm has learnt people from these countries pay more. The solution is to book from a local wifi connection - but a different one from the one you originally searched from.

How to get last-minute discounts on owner rented properties

In addition to Airbnb, you can also find owner rented rooms and apartments on www.vrbo.com or HomeAway or a host of others. Nearly all owners renting accommodation will happily give renters a "last-minute" discount to avoid the space sitting empty, not earning a dime.

Go to Airbnb or another platform and put in today's date. Once you've found something you like start the negotiating by asking for a 25% reduction. A sample message to an Airbnb host might read:

Dear HOST NAME,

I love your apartment. It looks perfect for me. Unfortunately, I'm on a very tight budget. I hope you won't be offended, but I wanted to ask if you would be amenable to offering me a 25% discount for tonight, tomorrow and the following day? I see that you aren't booked. I can assure you, I will leave your place exactly the way I found it. I will put bed linen in the washer and ensure everything is clean for the next guest. I would be delighted to bring you a bottle of wine to thank you for any discount that you could offer.

If this sounds okay, please send me a custom offer, and I will book straight away.

YOUR NAME.

In my experience, a polite, genuine message like this, that proposes reciprocity will be successful 80% of the time. Don't ask for more than 25% off, this person still has to pay the bills and will probably say no as your stay will cost them more in bills than they make. Plus starting higher, can offend the owner and do you want to stay somewhere, where you have offended the host?

In Practice

To use either of these methods, you must travel light. Less stuff means greater mobility, everything is faster and you don't have to check-in or store luggage. If you have a lot of luggage, you're going to have fewer of these opportunities to save on accommodation. Plus travelling light benefits the planet - you're buying, consuming, and transporting less stuff.

Blind-booking

If your risk tolerance does not allow for last-minute booking, you can use blind-booking. Many hotels not wanting to cheapen their brand with known low-prices, choose to operate a blind booking policy. This is where you book without knowing the name of the hotel you're going to stay in until you've made the payment. This is also sometimes used as a marketing strategy where the hotel is seeking to recover from past issues. I've stayed in plenty of blind book hotels. As long as you choose 4 or 5 star hotels, you will find them to be clean, comfortable and safe. priceline.com, Hot Rate® Hotels and Top Secret Hotels (operated by lastminute.com) offer the best deals.

Hotels.com Loyalty Program

This is currently the best hotel loyalty program with hotels in Florence. The basic premise is you collect 10 nights and get 1 free. hotels.com price match, so if booking.com has a cheaper price you can get hotel.com, to match. If you intend to travel more than ten nights in a year, its a great choice to get the 11th free.

Don't let time use you.

Rigidity will cost you money. You pay the price you're willing to pay, not the amount it requires a hotel to deliver. Therefore if you're in town for a big event, saving money on accommodation is nearly impossible so in such cases book three months ahead.

The best price performance location in Florence

A room putting Florence's attractions, restaurants, and nightlife are within walking distance will save you time on transport. However, Restaurants and bars get much cheaper the further you go from famous tourist attractions. You will also get a better idea of the day to day life of a local if you stay in a neighbourhood like Careggi Rifredi. It depends on the Florence you want to experience. For the tourist experience stay in the centre either in a last-minute hotel or Airbnb. For a taste of local life the leafy district of Careggi Rifredi is the best you will find. Hotel Raffaello is a luxurious four-star hotel with last-minute rooms from $60 a night.

Use our FREE accommodation finder service

Feeling overwhelmed by all the accommodation options? Save yourself stress, hassle and time by using our FREE accommodation finder service.

We pride ourselves on actively helping our readers find the best price-performance accommodation. We normally charge $50 for this service, but for our paid readers it is FREE when you leave an honest review of this book. (Just a few short words like 'Excellent budget tips and insider insights' is all it takes).

So, how do you use the service?

Simply send our Services Manager, Amy Abraham the following information:

1. A screenshot proof of purchase. (Go to your Amazon account, and click orders and make a screenshot of your purchase.)
2. Send a screenshot of your review of the guide on Amazon.
3. And answers to the following questions:

- What's your Budget? (e.g. lowest possible)
- How many are travelling and what are their ages?
- What Approximate location do you desire? (e.g. as close to the centre as possible/ near public transport)
- Do you have a strong dislike of either hostels or Airbnbs?

- If anyone in your group has mobility restrictions/ requires a lift/ no stairs etc?
- Add any details you think are pertinent to your needs.

About Amy and her team

Amy has travelled to over 170 countries personally and has recruited a team of bargain hunters to provide our accommodation finder service.

Send your details via E-mail to Amy Abraham at Amy@supercheapinsiderguides.com

What you'll receive

Amy and her team will work their magic. Within 24 hours you will be sent a list of the top three accommodations for your specific needs prioritised by which one we recommend.

We offer the same service for finding you the cheapest most direct flight. See our cheapest route to Florence for details.

If you would like to follow us on Facebook you can find us here: https://www.facebook.com/SuperCheapInsiderGuides/ . We also accept accommodation search requests via Facebook messenger, just make sure you send the necessary information listed above.

(Please note: If you received this book for free as part of a promotion, we cannot extend this service to you.)

How to be a green tourist in Florence

Florence like other major cities struggles with air pollution, so its important as responsible tourists that we help not hinder Florence.

There is a bizarre misconception that you have to spend money to travel in an eco-friendly way. This like, all marketing myths was concocted and hyped by companies seeking to make money off of you. In my experience, anything with eco in front of their names e.g Eco-tours will be triple the cost of the regular tour. Don't get me wrong sometimes its best to take these tours if you're visiting endangered areas, but normally such places have extensive legislation that everyone, including the eco and non-eco tour companies, are complying with. The vast majority of ways you can travel eco-friendly are free and even save you money.

- Avoid Bottled Water - get a good water bottle and refill. The water in Florence is safe to drink.
- Thrift shop but check the labels and don't buy polyester clothes - overtime plastic is released into the ocean when we wash polyester.
- Don't put it in a plastic bag, bring a cotton tote with you when you venture out.
- Pack Light - this is one of the best ways to save money. If you find a 5-star hotel for tonight for $10, and you're at an Airbnb or hostel, you can easily pack and upgrade hassle-free. A light pack equals freedom and it means less to wash.
- Travel around Florence on Bikes or e-Scooters or use Public Transportation.
- Car Pool with services like bla bla car or Uber/Lyft share.
- Walk, this is the best way to get to know Florence. You never know what's around the corner.

- Travel Overland - this isn't always viable especially if you only have limited time off work, but where possible avoid flying and if you have to compensate by off-setting or keeping the rest of your trip carbon-neutral by doing all of the above.

Saving money on Florence Food

Use 'Too Good To Go'

Florence offers plenty of food bargains; if you know where to look. Thankfully the app 'Too Good to Go' is turning visitors into locals by showing them exactly where to find the tastiest deals and simultaneously rescue food that would otherwise be wasted. In Florence you can pick up a $15 buy of baked goods, groceries, breakfast, brunch, lunch or dinner boxes for $2.99. You'll find lots of fish and meat dishes on offer in Florence, which would normally be expensive.

How it works? You pay for a magic bag (essentially a bag of what the restaurant or bakery has leftover) on the app and simply pick it up from the bakery or restaurant during the time they've selected. You can find extremely cheap breakfast, lunch, dinner and even groceries this way. Simply download the app and press 'my current location' to find the deals near you in Florence. https://toogoodtogo.org/en .What's not to love about restaurant quality delicious food thats a quarter of the normal price and helping to drive down food waste?

An oft-quoted parable is 'There is no such thing as cheap food. Either you pay at the cash registry or the doctor's office'. This dismisses the fact that good nutrition is a choice; we all make every-time we eat. Cheap eats are not confined to hotdogs and kebabs. The great thing about using Too Good To Go is you can eat nutritious food cheaply: fruits, vegetables, fish and nut dishes are a fraction of their supermarket cost.

Japan has the longest life expectancy in the world. A national study by the Japanese Ministry of Internal Affairs and Communications revealed that between January and May 2019, a household of two spent on average ¥65,994 a month, that's $10 per person per day on food. You truly don't need to spend a lot to eat nutritious food. That's a marketing gimmick hawkers of overpriced muesli bars want you to believe.

Breakfast

If you stay somewhere with a free breakfast, eat smart. Don't eat sugary cereals or white flour rich pastries if you don't want to be hungry an hour later. Before leaving your hotel or checking out, find some fresh fruit, water, and granola in the fitness centre or coffee in the lobby or business centre. If your hotel doesn't have free breakfast, don't take it. You can always eat cheaper outside. Caffè Rosanò has the best cheap breakfast we found. Here you can pick up a croissant and coffee for less than $4.

Visit supermarkets at discount times.

You can get a 50 per cent discount around 5 pm at the Conad and Coop supermarkets on fresh produce. The cheaper the supermarket, the less discounts you will find, so check Conad and Coop at 5 pm before checking the discount markets. Some items are also marked down due to sell-by date after the lunchtime rush so its also worth to check in around 3 pm.

Use delivery services on the cheap.

Take advantage of local offers on food delivery services. Most platforms including Deliveroo offer $10 off the first order in Florence.

SNAPSHOT: How to enjoy a $1,000 trip to Florence for $172

(full breakdown at the end of the guide)

Stay	Stay in hostels if you want to meet over travellers. The best price performance hostel is Santa Monica Hostel. Or there's the option to use our free accommodation finder service.
Eat	You don't need to spend a fortune in Florence to eat memorable food. Average meal cost: $6 - $10 for cheap eats
Move	Walk or use local buses
See	Cathedral of Santa Maria del Fiore and Piazza Duomo. Battistero di San Giovanni (Baptistery of St. John) Uffizi Palace and Gallery. Galleria dell'Accademia. You can get away with visiting all of these for under $35
Total	US$172

Unique bargains I love in Florence

The city feels like you're walking through a museum and the walking is free, so is gazing at all the stunning architecture! There are street performers everywhere providing free shows (just watch out for pickpockets). You can visit all the museums for free on the first Sunday of every month. And a bottle of chianti wine can be as cheap as $2 and is delicious. Take advantage of free snacks around the city during the aperitivo hours of 7 - 9pm. And get ready to eat your body weight in cheap delicious Tuscan sandwiches! Even the most reluctant bargain hunter can be successful in Florence. There's so much to see and do cheaply that you will be planning your second visit.

Take your student card
Florence offers hundreds of student discounts. If you're studying buy an ISIC card - International Student Identity Card. It's a great investment because its valid in 133 countries and covers 150,000 discounts including many hundreds in Florence.

How to use this book

Google and Tripadvisor are your on-the-go guides while travelling, a travel guide adds the most value during the planning phase, and if you're without wifi. Always download the google map for your destination - having an offline map will make using this guide much more comfortable. For ease of use, we've set the book out the way you travel starting with arriving, how to get around, then on to the money-saving tips. The tips we ordered according to when you need to know the tip to save money, so free tours and combination tickets feature first. We prioritised the rest of the tips by how much money you can save and then by how likely it was that you would be able to find the tip with a google search. Meaning those we think you could find alone are nearer the bottom. I hope you find this layout useful. If you have any ideas about making Super Cheap Insider Guides easy to use, please email me
philgtang@gmail.com

A quick note on how we Source Super Cheap Tips

We focus entirely on finding the best bargains. We give each of our collaborators $2,000 to hunt down never-before-seen deals. The type you either only know if you're local or by on the ground research. The actual writing and editing are done for free by four people (see who are writers are at the end of the book). As we grow, we will hire more writers to pen fabulous prose, but for now, we are in the nuts and bolts of hunting down unbelievable deals. We do this yearly, which means we just keep finding more amazing ways for you to have the same experience for less, but that's also why if you read or listen more of our guides, you may find the sentence structure familiar. Like many other guide book companies (Lonely Planet, Rough Guides etc) we use a content management system (ie, we repurpose some text). We'd like to be upfront about this so if you read or listen to another of our guides you aren't annoyed. Its worth mentioning that we pride ourselves on being a hands-on travel guide, and we put substantial resource behind helping you find the cheapest flight (explained in a moment) and the best value accommodation.

Another way you can save and make money is to apply to become one of our local collaborators at supercheapinsiderguides.com. We require you to identify a minimum of 250 super cheap tips and you need to live in the area you research. When you hear INSIDER HISTORICAL INSIGHT or INSIDER CULTURAL INSIGHT or INSIDER MONEY SAVING TIP this is a specific tip our insider contributed. Now let's get started with juicing the most pleasure from your trip to Florence with the least possible money.

OUR SUPER CHEAP TIPS...

Here are our specific super cheap tips for enjoying a $1,000 trip to Florence for just $172.

Cheapest route to Florence from America

At the time of writing Norwegian are flying to Florence for $168 out of Miami. Phil's day job for the past 15 years has been finding cheap flights for blue chip companies, so if you need help finding a cheap flight Phil can help you for free. Simply review this book and send him an email. philgtang@gmail.com (Please send a screenshot of your review - with your flight hacking request). Phil aims to reply to you within 12 hours. If it's an urgent request mark the email URGENT in the subject line and he will endeavour to reply ASAP.

If you are flying from elsewhere Phil can also help you find the cheapest direct flight to Florence for free. Just e-mail.

Arriving

If you arrive by bus or train, the orange ATAF Volainbus bus shuttle is the cheapest way to the city, it takes about 20 minutes, runs every half an hour and costs 5 euros. It leaves from the SITA bus station near the SMN railway station and from near the taxi rank at the station itself.

Coming in by plane? You can also take the ATAF Volainbus bus shuttle. The airport is just 4km from the centre of Florence.

Parking is a nightmare in Florence. Don't drive unless you have no other choice.

Getting around

The best way to get around Florence is by foot. You can walk from one end of the city to the other in about 30 minutes, passing many recognisable sites along the way. Hopping aboard an ATAF bus is another option but will set you back 7.50 euros a journey. You can also take one of the hop-on/hop-off buses that will get you between major attractions but these aren't cheap, costing

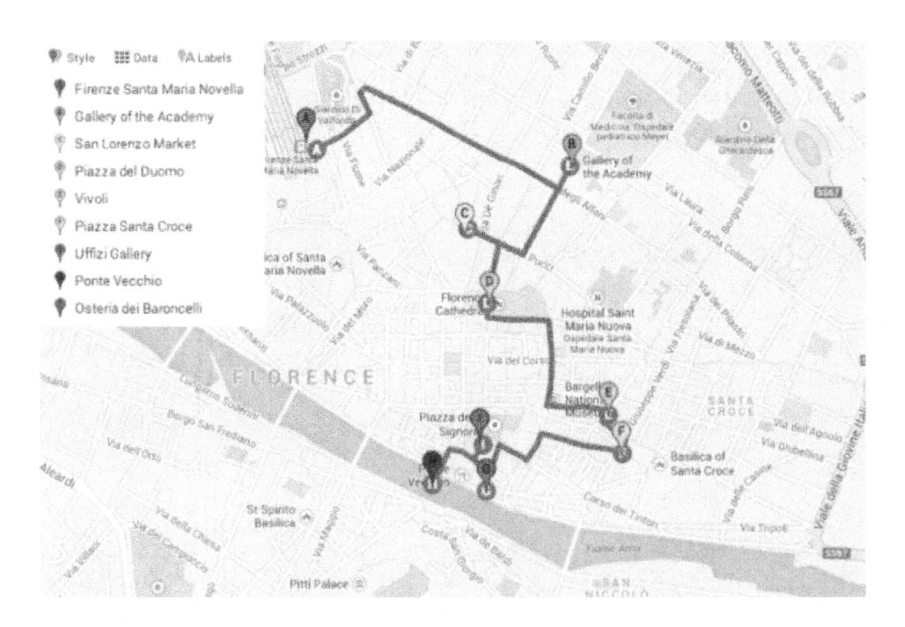

€23 for 24 hours per person.

Orientate yourself with this free tour

Forget exploring the city by wandering around aimlessly. Start with a free organised tour. Nothing compares to local advice, especially when travelling on a budget. Ask for their recommendations for the best cheap eats, the best bargains, the best markets, the best place for a particular street eat. Perhaps some of it will be repeated from this guide, but it can't hurt to ask, especially if you have specific needs or questions. At the end you should leave an appropriate tip (usually around $5), but nobody bats an eye lid if you are unable or unwilling to do so, tell them you will leave a good review and always give them a little gift from home - I always carry small Vienna fridge magnets and I always tip the $5, but it is totally up to you.

This is the free tour I did. I thought it was a great introduction to the vast history of Florence and covered the main attractions including a look at a leather workshop. You can book here: http://www.florence-freewalkingtour.com/tours/

A note on paying for tours

The only time paying for a tour is worth it, is when you couldn't reach the place without the tour (e.g you need a boat), or when the tour is about the same price as the attraction entry. Otherwise you can do a range of self-guided tours using gpsmycity.com for FREE.

💡 INSIDER MONEY SAVING TIP

If you have time Try Geocaching. This is where you hunt for hide-and-seek containers. You need a mobile device to follow the GPS clues. A typical cache is a small, waterproof container with a logbook where you can leave a message or other various sentiments or trinkets left by other cache searchers. Build your own treasure hunt by discovering geocaches in Florence. www.geocaching.com

Consider the Firenzecard

Museum aficionados can save money with the Firenzecard - The official museum pass of City of Florence. The card costs 85 euros, it is valid for 72 hours from the first entrance and you can enter 76 museums for free. It only becomes a good investment if a, you're short on time or b, you plan to see at least 10 paid museums/attractions.

No time to wait in line?

In July, August and Easter queues to the most popular musei statali (state museums) can be up to 4 hours. Save yourself from having a meltdown, literally and figuratively, by pre-booking your ticket. For a fee of € 3 per ticket (€ 4 for the Uffizi and Galleria dell'Accademia), Palazzo Pitti, Museo del Bargello and the Medicean chapels (Cappelle Medicee).

If you plan to visit Uffizi and Accademia during these times pre-booking is vital. To book your ticket go to:

Accademia ((where David lives): http://www.accademia.org/buy-tickets/

Uffizi: https://www.uffizi.it/en/tickets

Book this incredible secret tour

For for 5 euros (2 euros for children) you can do a secret passages tour of Palazzo Vecchio. We were shown the hidden passages in a walls starting from the outside of the palace, treasury rooms and the roof and attic of a palazzo never opened for public access. The tour started at 4.30 and lasted for 1hr 30 min but times defer year round. It is a total bargain. Be careful when booking it, lots of people are reselling it at much higher prices. Only buy from http://musefirenze.it/en/.

When you book you will get this message: Please come to the Info Point desk next to Palazzo Vecchio ticket office's museum 15 minutes in advance, to purchase and collect your ticket and wait for your guide. You will pay at arrival.

Make sure you book in advance, it gets booked up!

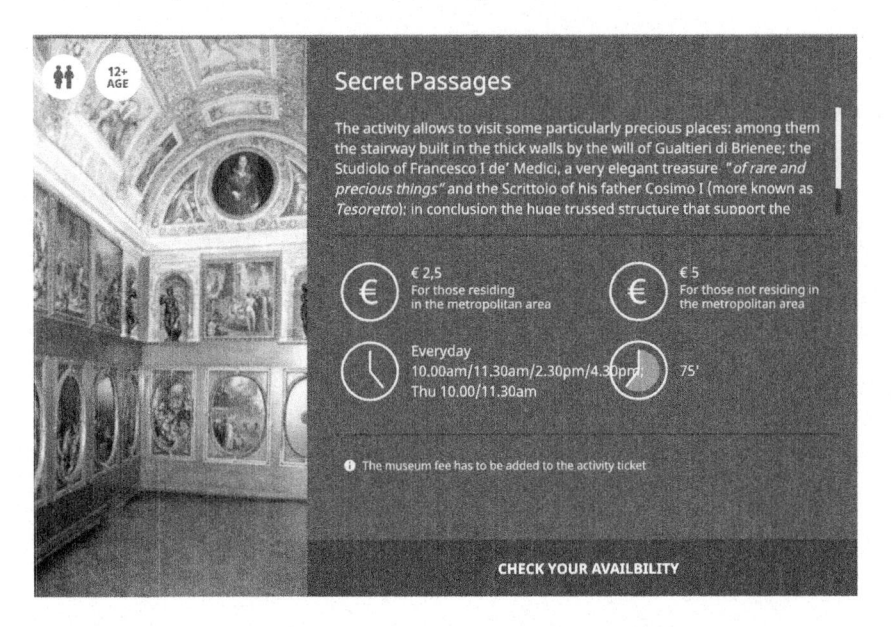

Secret Passages

The activity allows to visit some particularly precious places: among them the stairway built in the thick walls by the will of Gualtieri di Brienee; the Studiolo of Francesco I de' Medici, a very elegant treasure *"of rare and precious things"* and the Scrittoio of his father Cosimo I (more known as *Tesoretto*); in conclusion the huge trussed structure that support the

€ 2,5 — For those residing in the metropolitan area
€ 5 — For those not residing in the metropolitan area

Everyday
10.00am/11.30am/2.30pm/4.30pm;
Thu 10.00/11.30am
75'

ⓘ The museum fee has to be added to the activity ticket

CHECK YOUR AVAILBILITY

Visit these Amazing Museums for free

On the **first Sunday of the month** admission to state museums, including the Uffizi and Galleria dell'Accademia, is **FREE**! If you can time your trip right you can save a small fortune.

The Last Suppers and Cloisters
These are smaller State-run museums which comprise a small area within cloisters/churches and are all free entrance.

- 'Cenacolo' of Ognissanti - Last Supper of Ognissanti
- 'Cenacolo' of Andrea del Sarto - Last Supper of San Salvi
- 'Cenacolo' of Fuligno
- 'Cenacolo' of Sant'Apollonia - Last Supper of Sant'Apollonia
- Cloister of the Scalzo

Il Duomo di Firenz

The Il Duomo di Firenze (also called Santa Maria del Fiore) or Florence Cathedral was erected in 1296, it took over 150 years to build, it is a stunning white, green and pink marble façade with enormous doors. Standing at 114 meters tall it's is viewable from nearly every part of the city. Admiring the the outside will be one of the jaw-dropping moments of your trip to Florence. You can see the interior for free, though it doesn't match the exterior in grandiosity, and you will have a long wait in.

If you want to see the view from the Duomo for €15 you can access 5 monuments in Piazza Duomo (dome, bell tower, baptistery, crypt below cathedral, and Opera del Duomo Museum).

💡 INSIDER TIP
Climb the Giotto's Bell Tower instead of Il Duomo - climbing the bell tower is easier, and you get a view of the Duomo super close up.

Opposite the Duomo is **The Baptistry** an oval-shaped building dating back to the 12th century. For 3 euros you can go inside to see its frescoes and golden mosaics that will leave you mesmerised. Open Mon-Sat 12pm to 6.30pm, Sun 8.30am-1.30pm.

Go to the oldest art gallery in the world

The Uffizi Gallary was built in the 16th century, it is full of priceless Italian paintings and also Italy's most important art gallery. However, the Uffizi Gallary is on EVERYONE'S agenda so 2-5 hours lines are very common so PRE-BOOK YOUR TICKETS.

Visit David at Accademia

The Galleria dell'Accademia (Accademia Gallery) is the best sculpture gallery most famous for its sculptures by Michelangelo — his David statue - the most famous sculpture in the world is here. It took Michelangelo three years of carving from his marble block until David was seen. Again, book tickets online in advance. If you don't want to pay to see the statue of David... you can see the most similar replica in Piazza della Signoria.

Bargello Museum

Also known as the Palazzo del Bargello, Museo Nazionale del Bargello, or Palazzo del Popolo is not as well known as some of Florence's other museums, the Bargello has the largest collection of Italian sculptures from the 14th to the 16th centuries.
The price of entry is worth it to see the building. There are works from Donatello, Della Robbia, Cellini, Giambologna, and Michelangelo. No need to pre-book, the lines are never that bad. Tickets are 9 euros.

Basilica di Santa Croce

A beautiful church that houses the tombs of Michelangelo and Galileo. The basilica itself is majestic, with the front overlaid with white, pink and green marble and a cenotaph honouring Dante. There is no charge to enjoy the mass (7:30 - 9:00pm), otherwise it's 8€ to enter. The Tomb of Michelangelo Buonarroti, Basilica of Santa Croce, Florence. Michelangelo's Tomb is a work of Vasari (1570) and it's found at the beginning of the right aisle of the church of Santa Croce, just inside the main door of the Basilica.

Palazzo Pitti

The Palazzo Pitti is a gallery complex in a Renaissance royal palace house with a vast Italian & European masters art collection. The entry ticket for all the museums of the Pitti Palace is € 8,50 (reduced price € 4,25) and allows you to visit the Palatine Gallery, the Royal Apartments, the Treasury of Grand Dukes, the Museum of Costume and Fashion and the Gallery of Modern Art.

For another 10 euros you can go into The Boboli Gardens which are located behind the Pitti Palace. For almost four centuries it was the garden of the residence of the great dukes of Tuscany, and for a short period of the kings of Italy.

People Watch in Florence's Squares

The large classic Italian squares are great places to take a break and people watch. Piazza della Repubblica and Piazza di San Giovanni in the centre of the city are constantly buzzing, but the best place to sit down with an ice-cream and watch Florentine life go by is Piazza della Signoria.

Go Church Hopping

Most of Florence's churches are free to visit. The best known of these is of course the Il Duomo but there are others. Chiesa di Santo Spirito in Piazza Santo Spirito is one of the city's most beautiful examples of Renaissance architecture while Chiesa Santa Maria dei Ricci offVia Calzaiuoli is small but extremely beautiful. The best view in Florence Located just 20 minutes walk from the Ponte Vecchio, Piazzale Michelangelo affords visitors the best views of Tuscany's capital.

Visit the Best Markets

Florence markets are a fun and eye-opening plunge into local culture and, unless you succumb to the persistent vendors, it will cost you nothing.

Sant'Ambrogio Market is a Fresh food market where you can buy prosciutto and local cheese very **cheaply**. It's on Piazza Lorenzo Ghiberti and Closes at 2PM.

Mercatopoli Firenze Legnaia on Via Frà Diamante, 12/A is a great place to buy second hand goods or vintage furniture. It Closes at 1PM.

The Mercado Central, Florence's most famous market is an excellent place to grab a quick, tasty, and inexpensive meal.

The San Lorenzo Market has all kinds of souvenirs, leather goods, scarves, clothing, etc.

Loggia del Mercato Nuovo. was built in the 16th century as a market for fine goods. Now it's a popular area for tourists thanks to its many souvenir stalls and prices match its affluent past.

Don't be afraid of bargaining with vendors. You should aim to knock 30% off the price.

All markets can get crowded making them prime targets for pickpockets. Don't keep anything in your back pockets and keep an eye on your bag, wearing it on your front if it has pockets with easy access.

Parks and Gardens

The cost of eating out can quickly add up. For a meal that doesn't break the bank, prepare your own picnic with a bottle of chianti, some cheese, local breads and head to any of these free parks in walking distance of the centre:

- Parco delle Cascine
- Giardino dell'Orticultura
- Giardino delle Rose
- Parco di Villa il Ventaglio
- Giardini dell'Anconella and Parco dell'Albereta
- Parco di Villa Fabbricotti, Giardino Baden Powell and Giardino del Museo Stibbert

Parco delle Cascine above.

Go Thrift shopping

Thanks to its rich inhabitants Florence thrift and flea markets are packed full of Italian designer gems. If you're travelling light, which you should be to save money you can pick up a new outfit for under five dollars from. Rewind Vintage Selection is full of bargains. You can get stylish fashionable clothes selected by the owner carefully. They have accessories too - made from local leather and the prices are 5 to 15 euros. Much cheaper than the shops that cater to tourists.

Address: Via S. Gallo, 23
Open · Closes 7:30PM
Phone: +39 347 236 1176

Take a stroll

There is always something going on along or on the River Arno. Rowers row, footballers play and you can see otters swimming.

Visit Ponte Vecchio

This Medieval stone bridge is well-known for the numerous shops built into the bridge. It is the only bridge which survived the Nazi bombings in WWII. It's bright colour means it is distinctive from the rest of the bridges. In summer it's packed with free street performers.

Take a day trip to Pisa

The train from Florence to Pisa Centrale is 1 hour and 12 euros return when you book in advance making it an ideal day trip.
https://www.thetrainline.com/en/train-times/florence-to-pisa-centrale

If you want to see Pisa's cathedral for free, then visit on Sunday morning for mass when the €2 admission fee is waived. It's also free every day from November to the end of February. Stained glass, religious art and an intricately decorated ceiling are all part of the cathedral's stunning interior. Open daily Nov-Feb 10am-12.45pm & 2pm-5pm, Mar 10am-6pm, Apr-Sept 10am-8pm, Oct 10am-7pm; admission free on Sunday mornings and daily from Nov-Feb.

Escape the crowds

Torrigiani Garden

If you are easily overwhelmed by crowds visit the obvious attractions as early as possible, peak people flow is 11 am to 5 pm so get up early to enjoy the attractions serenely. Luckily Florence also has many hidden gems that aren't commercialized or too crowded most of the time. Here are the best:

1. Villa Demidoff and the Park of Pratolino is a beautiful garden where a majestic 16th-century statue representing the Apennine Colosso dell'Appennino is hidden.
2. If you want to visit a museum without the crowds go to San Marco Museum. Hidden inside a Dominican monastery, the museum hosts beautiful pieces of art from the 16th-century.

3. Escape to Todo Modo a cozy bookstore in Florence with a great selection of English and Italian books and space to sit down and read.

4. Santa Maria Novella Pharmacy. Founded by Dominican friars in 1221, today you'll find perfumes instead of medicines.

6. Torrigiani Garden is a romantic English style garden and the largest private garden in Europe located within city boundaries. You need to book a free tour via email info@giardinotorrigiani.it Make sure you book before you travel.

7. Visit San Gimignano. It's busier than the other small medieval towns but in a good way. This small town is encircled by 13th-century walls, and offers a skyline of medieval towers.

8. The Best view over Florence is Piazzele Michelangelo- go at sunset and bring Champagne. It will be very crowded so walk down from the upper levels near the gate to the Rose Garden and watch sunset from there.

Nightlife

For a fun shot, go to Eby's Bar. The owner is a eccentric older gentleman and a complete blast.

Visit Off the Hook - Irish Bar with free live music and sweet bartenders.

Clubs: Babylon Club or YAB

If you go dancing, until about 3am, you can check out the Secret Bakery - its a bakery thats only open for one hour from 2 am - 3am. They keep the windows open and have no address, so you have to follow the smell of fresh pastries… It's located on a side street off of Via Ghibellina, opposite of the street that has Michelangelos house in it.

Don't leave Florence without seeing (even if only from outside)

Palazzo Vecchio
Fortified, 13th-century palace housing lavishly decorated chambers & ornate courtyards.

Piazza della Signoria
The city's heart, a square dominated by the 14th-century crenellated tower of the Palazzo Vecchio.

Piazzale Michelangelo
19th-century piazza with a bronze replica of Michelangelo's David & panoramic views over the city.

Santa Croce, Florence
Neo-Gothic Franciscan church known for its Giotto frescoes, plus tombs of Michelangelo & Galileo.

Giotto's Campanile
Celebrated red, green & white marble-clad Gothic tower with steps leading to a terrace & city views.

Piazza del Duomo, Florence
Cathedral-flanked square with monumental buildings designed by Giuseppe Nagoni in the 19th-century.

Santa Maria Novella
15th-century Dominican church including famous frescoes by Gothic & early Renaissance masters.

Museo dell'Opera del Duomo
Statues by Michelangelo & Donatello, plus bronze-gilded baptistery panels in a restoration center.

Basilica di San Lorenzo, Firenze
Landmark Renaissance church, burial place of the Medici, with a library designed by Michelangelo.

Piazza della Repubblica, Florence
Pedestrianized square lined with elegant cafes, also featuring a traditional merry-go-round.

Loggia dei Lanzi
14th-century ceremonial building with wide arches, an open-air gallery of Renaissance sculpture.

Vasari Corridor
The Vasari Corridor is an elevated enclosed passageway in Florence, central Italy, which connects the Palazzo Vecchio with the Palazzo Pitti. Beginning on the south side of the Palazzo Vecchio

Palazzo Medici Riccardi
15th-century palace designed by Michelozzo for the Medici family, with art museum & famous chapel.

Arno
The Arno is a river in the Tuscany region of Italy. It is the most important river of central Italy after the Tiber.

Santo Spirito, Florence
Brunelleschi's plain-fronted 1400s church with a lavish art-filled interior & baroque altar.

Fountain of Neptune, Florence
Octagonal fountain from the 16th century with a large statue of Neptune & other mythical figures.

Medici Chapel
Domed landmark containing tombs of the Medici family, including the New Sacristy by Michelangelo.

San Miniato al Monte
Hilltop, 11th-century church with a gleaming Romanesque facade, medieval interiors & city views.

Palazzo Strozzi
Renaissance palace with permanent display on its history, plus major temporary art exhibitions.

Giardino Bardini
Restored 17th-century villa set over 4 floors with 2 museums & art exhibitions, plus gardens.

Orsanmichele
Church & museum in a 14th-century granary with religious paintings & a marble shrine to the Madonna.

San Marco, Florence
Art museum in 15th-century convent housing Renaissance frescoes & 16th-century painting collection.

Porcellino
Visitors rub the snout of this iconic bronze fountain of a boar to ensure their return to Florence.

Museo Galileo
Collection of artifacts from the 15th/16th centuries, with scientific instruments & personal items.

Santa Croce
Lively Santa Croce centers on Basilica di Santa Croce, with its Giotto frescoes and monumental tombs of Michelangelo and Galileo.

Gates of Paradise
Famous golden doors of landmark Baptistery of St. John, with panels depicting Biblical scenes.

Ponte Santa Trinita
Delicate bridge with 3 arches, designed by Bartolomeo Ammanati & reconstructed after WWII.

Mercato di San Lorenzo
Iconic indoor/outdoor street market
Famous, bustling indoor/outdoor market of stalls selling local art, leather goods & regional foods.

Belvedere
1500s hilltop fortress offering sweeping vistas of the Florence skyline & frequent art exhibitions.

Palazzo Davanzati
Museum in 14th-century palazzo, filled with antiques, lace items & artworks, offering guided tours.

Santissima Annunziata, Florence

1200s Catholic church on an elegant square, rich in Renaissance art & landmark Mannerist frescoes.

Santa Trinita
Gothic-style church dotted with chapels, home to a landmark fresco cycle on the life of St. Francis.

Parco delle Cascine
This spacious riverfront park with many historical monuments is popular with runners & cyclists.

Ospedale degli Innocenti
Europe's oldest foundling hospital, with terracotta reliefs of babies by Andrea della Robbia.

National Archaeological Museum of Florence
Museum with Egyptian, Greek, Etruscan & Roman relics such as a rare chariot & bronze sculptures.

Giardino delle rose
Green space known for its rose terraces, plus a Japanese garden & sculptures by the artist Folon.

Is the tap water drinkable?

Yes.

How much can you save haggling here?

Haggling is common at markets in Florence. Haggling in stores is generally unacceptable, although some good-humoured bargaining at smaller artisan or craft shops in Italy is not unusual if you are making multiple purchases.

Food and drink hacks

Fill up your water bottle for free
The tap water in Florence is perfectly safe to drink. There is a water fountain right behind the Fountain of Neptune in the Piazza della Signoria for filling up your water bottle.

Coffee
If you stop in a café for a quick latté or espresso, make sure to drink it at the counter where it shouldn't cost more than €1. Take it outside to a table and you can add another €2 on top of that, just for sitting down, so learn to enjoy your coffee standing.

Aperitivo
Free snacks are distributed by bars from 7-9pm to entice you to buy more alcohol. Visit different bars, each will put out a different snack.

Best bang for your buck all-you-can-eat
Aji Tei is a Japenese all you can eat loved by locals for a $12 lunch.
Address: Viale Spartaco Lavagnini, 20A

The best gelato

Some of the best ice-cream I have ever tasted is available at **DONDURMACI Gelateria Della Passera** and its cheap! They have an inspiring selection of flavors, each offering a true gelato experience.

Address : Via Toscanella, 15 / red
Open Closes 8:30 PM

Must-try Florence food

Florence food is a smorgasbord of culture and history. Here are the best morsels you should try (apologies to vegetarians and vegans - local cuisine is meat heavy):

- Bistecca alla Fiorentina is a Steak that historically came from a Tuscan cattle, called the Chianina. This breed of cattle is known for their incredibly flavorful meat.
- Lampredotto is another cow dish (sorry veggies and vegans, Florentines love meat) this one is made from the stomach.
- Papardelle al Cinghiale is a homemade pasta in wild boar sauce.
- Tagliatelle Funghi Porcini e Tartufo, finally a veggie meal. This is tagliatelle with mushrooms and truffles.
- Crostini (Antipasto Toscano) is a tuscan style bruschetta.
- Ribollita and Pappa al Pomodoro is a soup made with bread, tomatoes, beans and many vegetables.
- Pane Toscano is widely popular Tuscan unsalted bread.

These are the top best wines to try in Florence (Mercato Centrale is the cheapest place to try them):

- Chianti, start with the Chianti classico
- Rosso di Montalcino
- Brunello di Montalcino

You can easily do your own DIY wine tasting by picking up a bottle of each at a supermarket.

Cheap Eats

It's actually quite hard to have a bad meal in Florence, but it's easy to have an overpriced one. Fill your stomach without emptying your wallet. Get a taste of the city's most authentic flavours for the lowest price at these local restaurants with mains under $12:

Note: Download the offline map for Florence on Google maps, (instructions 1. go to app 2. select offline apps in the left sidebar 3. go to the area you want to download 4. click download). Then simply type the restaurant names in to navigate, add the restaurants to your favourites by clicking the star icon so you can see where the cheap eats are when you're out and about to avoid wasting your money at hyped tourist joints)

Acqua al Due
Try the Balsamic glazed steak and house red wine. You can also get a pasta or meat tasting entree, where they bring out 5 small portions of different flavored pastas that equal to one full portion - fun with groups and less than $15.

Santo Sporito
For a super chill dinner, you can check out the neighborhood across the river. In the main piazza near Santo Sporito church, you can find Gusta Pizza, a famous to-go pizza joint, and grab some wine to go and eat it on the steps of the church surrounded by mostly locals.

All'Antico Vinaio
Sandwich - Great for a cheap but filling sandwich on the go.
Address: Via dei Neri, 74/R

Aurelio, the King of Lampredotto
Cheap delicious wild boar sandwiches.
Address: Piazza Bernardo Tanucci

Trattoria La Casalinga
All the pasta dishes was delicious, the prices were cheap.
Address: Via dei Michelozzi, 9/R

Pane & Toscana
Cheap meal with delicious food.
Address: Borgo degli Albizi, 31

Mangia Pizza Firenze
The best pizza for the lowest price.
Address: Via Lambertesca, 24/26/R

Da' Vinattieri
Delicious cheap eats, better than anything you'll get off the main street.
Address: Via Santa Margherita, 4/R

Il Cernacchino
Really cheap delicious sandwich place.
Address: Via della Condotta, 38R

Trattoria Sostanza
Great Food and where the locals go to eat.
Address: Via del Porcellana, 25/R

Trattoria Mario
Good tuscan food, nice service, and quite cheap. Note: arrive early
Address: Via Rosina, 2r

Sergio Pollini Lampredotto
Fast Food place with sandwiches
Address: Via dei Macci, 126

Cash only · Casual

Pino's Sandwiches - Salumeria Verdi
delicious sandwiches and pasta.. cheap! friendly staff
Address: Via Giuseppe Verdi, 36//R

Nobile Bistrò
Address: Piazza di Madonna degli Aldobrandini, 13
Great service, super friendly owners and the food is cheap and delicious.

Trattoria Anita
Cheap, home cooked authentic tuscan food and you'll find mostly locals eating here.
Address: Via del Parlascio, 2

Le Volpi e l'Uva
Great wine selection and low prices.
Address: Piazza dei Rossi, 1R

l'Pizzacchiere
Delicious cheap Pizza joint.
Address: Via S. Miniato, 2

La Managere
Great if you want to visit an aesthetically beautiful cafe (either for coffee, breakfast (They have great avocado toast, brunch options and cappucino!) The Decor is simply beautiful. And they have Good cocktails too.

Avoid any restaurant near attractions or with touts outside. It will be overpriced and low quality. Instead look out for 'Trattorias' these are lower cost restaurants. You can also pick up huge sandwiches and pizza's for under $5 if you're on a tight budget.

Save money on restaurants cafes with these tips

Any bar or cafe has to have their prices posted by law in Italy. And they'll have two: bar and table. If you want to save money on eating out, take away the food or drinks. This goes for coffee too. An espresso at the bar costs 1 euro. It will cost you 3 euros to drink it sitting down. All Italian restaurants charge a cover charge for the bread, oil, napkins etc, normally 3 euros.

Buy soda at the supermarket not the restaurant. A small can will cost at least 5 Euros at a restaurant.

Don't ask your waiter to recommend a wine, he will recommend the most expensive.

Fish: often fish is listed on the menu by weight so what looks like a $7 fish is probably more like 35 euros for the whole fish.

Need to Know before you go

Currency: Euro

Language: Italian

Money: Widely available ATMs. Beware American Express might not work here.

Visas: check http://www.doyouneedvisa.com/

Time: GMT + 1

When to Go

High Season: July and August.

Shoulder: May, April, June

Low Season: September to May.

Important Numbers

113 Ambulance

112 Police

History documentary

Florence 's history is fascinating. There are tons of documentaries. History Summarized: Florence is a great one to watch before your visit. Just type it into YouTube to watch.

Language

Here are some Practical Italian phrases that are easy to remember to help you save money, make friends and avoid annoying the locals.

Hello	Ciao
Yes	Sì
No	No
How much?	Quanto?
Discount?	Sconto?
I am on a budget	Ho un budget
I am from _____	Vengo da _____
My name is	Il mio nome è
How to I find the train / metro / bus?	Come trovo il treno / metro / autobus?
I would like a beer, please.	Vorrei una birra, per favore.
Where is the bathroom?	Dov'è il bagno?
Can you show me on this map?	Può mostrarmelo su questa mappa?
Where is _____?	Dove si trova _____?
I'm lost.	Mi sono perso.
Do you speak English?	Parli inglese?
Can you speak slower?	Puoi parlare più lentamente?
Do you have WIFI?	Hai il WIFI?
What is the WIFI password?	Qual è la password WIFI?
Sorry	Scusa
Thank you	Grazie
Goodbye	Addio
Please	Per favore
Good Evening	Buona sera

Getting Out of Florence cheaply

Train

Italia Trains operates services to Pisa for $15 return. Check their website for other destinations and the best deals but also cross check for the lowest price using goeuro.com

Bus

Bus Italia is the cheapest option for onward buses from Florence. Booking ahead can save you up to 98% of the cost of the ticket.

Plane

At the time of writing Austria Airlines are offering the cheapest flights onwards from Florence. Take advantage of discounts and specials. Sign up for e-newsletters from local carriers including Austria Airlines to learn about special fares. It is much cheaper to fly from nearby Pisa.

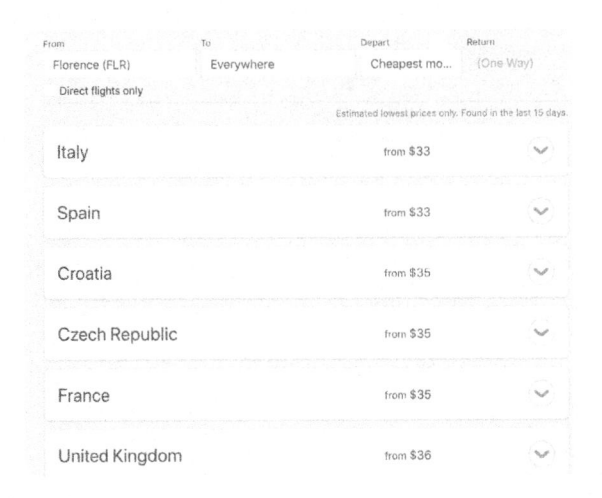

From	To	Depart	Return
Florence (FLR)	Everywhere	Cheapest mo...	(One Way)
Direct flights only			

Estimated lowest prices only. Found in the last 15 days.

Italy	from $33
Spain	from $33
Croatia	from $35
Czech Republic	from $35
France	from $35
United Kingdom	from $36

Avoid these tourist traps or scams

The only real issue in Florence is pickpockets. They operate in crowded areas. Don't keep anything in your back pockets and use a day bag that's not easy to open. Pickpockets target tourists in Florence. Disguise yourself as a local by buying a local branded reusable supermarket bag to use as your day bag.

There are also some "Friendship" Bracelet operators. A vendor approaches you and aggressively asks if you'll help him with a "demonstration." He proceeds to make a friendship bracelet right on your arm. When finished, he asks you to pay a premium for the bracelet he created just for you. And, since you can't easily take it off on the spot, you feel obliged to pay up. (These sorts of distractions by "salesmen" can also function as a smokescreen for theft — an accomplice is picking your pocket as you try to wriggle away from the pushy vendor.)

Don't sit down to have your coffee - this will cost you three times more. And avoid eating at any restaurant you haven't checked carefully on Tripadvisor. The restaurants I included above all have mains under 8 euros, it's worth to star some places you want to eat at before your trip so you don't give in to hunger and go to a place that will rip you off.

RECAP: How to have a $1,000 trip to Florence on a $172 budget

Five star hotels
Book Last minute 5 star hotel deals. Check on the same day of your stay for cheap five star hotel deals. Go to booking.com enter Florence, tonight, only one night and filter by 5 stars. This can be very effective in the low season when hotels empty of travellers. Potential saving $800.

Pick-up Cheap food
Install the 'Too Good To Go' app to get amazing food super cheap. Potential saving $150.

Restaurant deals
A lot of restaurants in Florence offer a midday menu for lunch at around 8.90€. If you're on a budget, but like eating out, consider doing your dining in the daytime.
Potential saving $100.

Go to museums/ attractions on their free days
The average traveller spends $130 on museums in Florence but there's no need to if you visit on the first Sunday when most are free and start early to see all the museums for free. If you can't time your trip to include a first Sunday buy the Firenze card. Potential saving $130.

Book buses/ flights early
Book your onward transport 6 weeks before you travel to get the lowest prices especially on flights, buses or blablacars journeys. Potential saving $100.

Fully costed Breakdown

	How	Cost normally	Cost when following suggested tip
How I got from the airport to the city	bus -	$25 Taxi	5 euros
Where I stayed	Hostel Santa Monaca $20 a night	Hotels are upwards of $150 a night. Airbnbs in the city don't come any cheaper than $45 a night.	$60
Tastiest street foods I ate and cost	Wild boar sandwiches and Chianti wine are centrale Mercado.	You can eat well in Florence for $6 - $10 a meal. Lunches are cheaper, and take advance of free apprevito snacks	$5 for the sandwiches. i spent $20 a day on food, so $60 total.
How I got around	Walked	Florence is compact, you can walk around it easily.	$0
What I saw and paid	Churches, museums, markets, galleries, the river.	I spent $45 on entering three museums: Uffizi, academia and the pitti palace.	$35
My onward flight	London from Pisa airport with Ryanair	Book six weeks ahead for the cheapest prices.	$12
My Total costs	US$172		US$172

The secret to saving HUGE amounts of money when travelling to Florence is...

Your mindset. Money is an emotional topic, if you associate words like cheapskate, Miser (and its £9.50 to go into Charles Dickens London house, oh the Irony) with being thrifty when travelling you are likely to say 'F-it' and spend your money needlessly because you associate pain with saving money. You pay now for an immediate reward. Our brains are prehistoric; they focus on surviving day to day. Travel companies and hotels know this and put trillions into making you believe you will be happier when you spend on their products or services. Our poor brains are up against outdated programming and an onslaught of advertisements bombarding us with the message: spending money on travel equals PLEASURE. To correct this carefully lodged propaganda in your frontal cortex you need to imagine your future self.

Saving money does not make you a cheapskate. It makes you smart. How do people get rich? They invest their money. They don't go out and earn it; they let their money earn more money. So every time you want to spend money, imagine this: while you travel your money is working for you, not you for money. While you sleep the money you've invested is going up and up. That's a pleasure a pricey entrance fee can't give you. Thinking about putting your money to work for you tricks your brain into believing you are not withholding pleasure from yourself, you are saving your money to invest so you can go to even more amazing places. You are thus turning thrifty travel into a pleasure fueled sport.

When you've got money invested - If you want to splash your cash on a first-class airplane seat - you can. I can't tell you how to invest your money, only that you should. Saving $20 on taxi's doesn't seem like much but over time you could be saving upwards of $15,000 a year, which is a deposit for a house which you can rent on Airbnb to finance more travel. Your brain making money looks like your brain on cocaine, so tell yourself saving money is making money.

Scientists have proved that imagining your future self is the easiest way to associate pleasure with saving money. You can download FaceApp — which will give you a picture of what you will look like older and greyer, or you can take a deep breath just before spending money and ask yourself if you will regret the purchase later.

The easiest ways to waste money travelling are:

Getting a taxi. The solution to this is to always download the google map before you go. Many taxi drivers will drive you around for 15 minutes when the place you were trying to get to is a 5-minute walk... remember while not getting an overpriced taxi to tell yourself, 'I am saving money to free myself for more travel.'
Spending money on overpriced food when hungry. The solution: carry snacks. A banana and an apple will cost you, in most places less than a dollar.
Spending on entrance fees to top-rated attractions. If you really want to do it, spend the money happily. If you're conflicted sleep on it. I don't regret spending $200 on a skydive over the Great Barrier Reef, I do regret going to the top of the shard in London for $60. Only you can know but make sure it's your decision and not the marketing directors at said top-rated attraction.
Telling yourself 'you only have the chance to see/eat/experience it now'. While this might be true, make sure YOU WANT to spend the money. Money spent is money you can't invest, and often you can have the same experience for much less.

You can experience luxurious travel on a small budget which will trick your brain into thinking you're already a high-roller, which will mean you'll be more likely to start acting like one and invest your money. Stay in five-star hotels for $5 by booking on the day of your stay on booking.com to enjoy last minute deals. You can go to fancy restaurants using daily deal sites. Ask your airline about last minute upgrades to first-class or business. I paid $100 extra on a $179 ticket to Cuba from Germany to be bumped to Business Class. When you ask you will be surprised what you can get both at hotels and airlines.

Travel, as the saying goes is the only thing you spend money on that makes you richer. In practice, you can easily waste money, making it difficult to enjoy that metaphysical wealth. The biggest money saving secret is to turn bargain hunting into a pleasurable activity, not an annoyance. Budgeting consciously can be fun, don't feel disappointed because you don't spend the $60 to go into an attraction, feel good because soon that $60 will soon be earning money for you. Meaning, you'll have the time and money to enjoy more metaphysical wealth, while your bank balance increases.

PRACTICAL THINGS TO REMEMBER TO SAVE MONEY IN FLORENCE

- Download google maps for for use offline - it will be easy to navigate Florence.
- Download the Italian Google translate offline pack. The camera function on Google Translate is great for translating Italian menus.
- Know the names of foods and wines to try
- Remember sitting down in restaurants or cafes adds service cover to your bill which is typically $3 per person. Get takeaway foods and eat on benches in the squares and drink your coffee standing up for a $1 cup compared to a $3 sat down.
- Don't eat at any restaurants with touts outside
- Go on the first Sunday of the month to go to all the state museums for free - but start at 7am, the crowds are real.
- Book your tickets to museums in advance to avoid the 4 hour lines!
- Plan to start sightseeing early for a more serene experience.
- Pick up food from the too good to go app - Plan to get your breakfast or dinner from restaurants on the app. $2.99 for a restaurant meal will save you at least $150 on the same quality food in Florence.
- Bring a good mosquito spray or combine a few drops of lemongrass oil with a moisturiser. This is the technique the Inca's used to keep mosquitos at bay. The smell turns the mosquitos away from your skin. Mosquitos can be a big nuisance in summer.
- Book any onward buses flights ahead to save.
- Bring an eye-mask and earplugs if you plan to stay in a hostel.
- Pack food for the airport, you'll save $10 on a bad cup of coffee and stale croissant.

- Avoid over-scheduling. You don't want to pack so much into your trip you wind up feeling like you're working on the conveyor belt called best sights of Florence instead of fully saturating your senses in the culture, Renaissance art, architecture, monuments and food.

So there it is, you can enjoy the best of Florence for less than $200 saving by being strategic with your trip planning. We've arranged everything in the guide to offer the best bang for your buck. Which means we took the view that if it's not a good investment for your money we wouldn't include it. Why would a guide called 'Super Cheap' include lots of overpriced attractions or tours? That said, if you think we've missed something or have unanswered questions just ping me an email philgtang@gmail.com I'm on central Europe time and normally reply within 8 hours of getting your mail.

Don't put your dreams off!

Time is a currency you never get back and travel is its greatest return on investment. Plus now you know you can visit Florence for a fraction of the price most would have you believe.

Websites to save you Money

1. **TalkTalkbnb.com** - Here you stay for free when you teach the host your native language
2. Rome2Rio.com - the go to site for good travel prices on train, bus, planes etc. Especially good for paths less travelled.
3. GoEuro.com - the best travel site in Europe.
4. couchsurfing.com - stay for free with a local - always check reviews.
5. trustedhousesitter.com - always check reviews
6. booking.com - now sends you vouchers for discounts in the city when you book through them
7. blablacar.com - travel in car with locals already going to your destination
8. airbnb.com for both accommodation and experiences.
9. hostelbookers.com - book hostels
10. http://www.florence-freewalkingtour.com/tours/ - free walking tour
11. When searching to buy tickets online always add 'Official website' to your search, many sneaky operators have constructed ticket purchasing sites which inflate the prices. ONLY BUY FROM THE OFFICIAL SITES.

Thank you for reading

Dear Lovely Reader,

If you have found this book useful, please consider writing a short review on Amazon.

One person from every 1000 readers leaves a review on Amazon. It would mean more than you could ever know if you were one of our 1 in 1000 people to take the time to write a short review.

We are a group of four friends who all met travelling 15 years ago. We believe that great experiences don't need to blow your budget, just your mind.

Thank you so much for reading again and for spending your time and investing your trips future in Super Cheap Insider Guides.

One last note, please don't listen to anyone who says 'Oh no, you can't visit Florence on a budget'. Unlike you they didn't have this book. The truth is you can do ANYWHERE on a budget with the right insider advice and planning. Sure, learning to travel to Florence on a budget that doesn't compromise on anything or drastically compromise on safety or comfort levels is a skill, but this guide has done the detective work for you. Now it is time for you to put the advice into action.

Phil

P.S If you need any more super cheap tips we'd love to hear from you e-mail me at philgtang@gmail.com, we have a lot of contacts in every region, so if there's a specific bargain you're hunting we can help you find it :-)

Are you visiting Rome on your Italy trip? Save more money with Super Cheap Rome.

SHOP 150 VACATIONS UNDER $150.

INCLUDING LONDON.

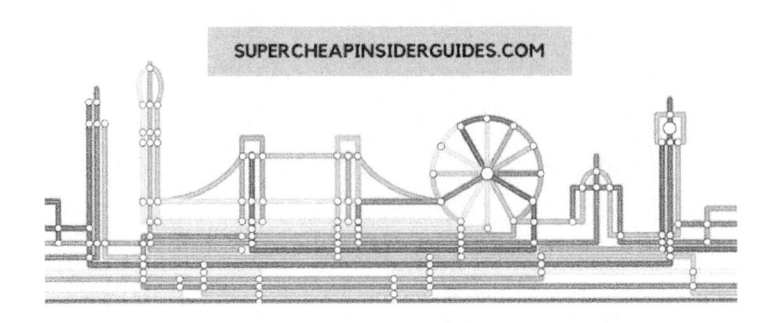

SUPERCHEAPINSIDERGUIDES.COM

UNCOVERED A SUPER CHEAP TIP DURING YOUR TRAVELS? GET PAID FOR IT. EMAIL PHILGTANG@GMAIL.COM

WE PAY FOR TIPS

CHOOSE FROM PRO RATA ROYALTIES OR A $50 AMAZON VOUCHER

Bonus Budget Travel Hacks

I've included these bonus travel hacks to help you plan and enjoy your trip to Florence cheaply, joyfully and smoothly. Perhaps they will even inspire you or renew your passion for long-term travel.

From saving space in your pack to scoring cheap flights, there are a wealth of generic travel hacks to help you enjoy stress-free, happier travels without breaking the bank. This is why I've included this bonus section to maximise the value you get from buying this book.

When I tell people I write a travel guide series focused on luxurious budget travel, they wrongly assume that's impossible and often say 'Hitchhiking and couch-surfing?'. Others with more vivid imaginations ask me if I recommend hooking up with older men or women... Of course, they are surprised when I tell them that not one of the 150 Super Cheap Guides endorses such practises because they maximise discomfort. They look at me dumbfounded and ask 'How on earth do you travel comfortably on a budget then?'

Travelling cheaply in a way that doesn't compromise enjoyment, comfort or safety is a skill I have honed over 20 years of travelling. My foremost learning was that locals always know the tricks and tips to enjoy the same or a better tourist experience for a 10th of the cost, and that's why I teamed up with locals in each locale to distil the tips that will save you a fortune without compromising on enjoyment or comfort.

Enjoyable budget travel is about balancing and prioritising what is important to you.
When I tell people about my methodology I often receive long defensive monologues about why they spend so much on travel, or why they can't or don't travel. Thats why we will first discuss how you can find the freedom to travel.

How to find the freedom to travel

> Freedom is one of those words that can mean different things to different people. It's important to be clear on what it looks like to you in your life, and all the stories and beliefs that prevent you from having it. For me, freedom means always having at choice in my life. I don't do anything that I don't want to do. —LEO BABAUTA

We've spoken a lot about how to save money travelling to Florence, but how do you find the freedom if you have:

1. Pets
2. Kids
3. A spouse who doesn't want you to travel
4. A job that keeps you at home?

Like everything, there's a solution to every problem. In this chapter, I want to you to think about whether your excuses can be overcome using the following solutions, because as Randy Komisar said: "And then there is the most dangerous risk of all – the risk of spending your life not doing what you want on the bet you can buy yourself the freedom to do it later."

Pets

I have a dog, an extremely loving German Shepherd. And when I travel overland from Austria she comes with me and my wife. If we are heading on a longer trip we either leave her with friends or family or we get someone to house sit for us. housesitters.com offers up people who are vetted and reviewed and in exchange for free accommodation will care for your pets. Just be aware it often works out financially better to rent your space on Airbnb and pay someone to look after your pets. Make sure you visit their facilities before you entrust your pet to anyone and of course, always read the reviews.

I know a lot of people miss their pets travelling which is why we endeavour to take our dog with us. Exploring with her has formed some of our most precious memories. If you're flying with your pet always look up the rules and make sure you comply. If you're going to the UK for example, they quarantine dogs who come in by air. So we only take our dog by car. Coming into the UK by car, dogs must need to be chipped, have a note from a vet saying they are clear of Rabies and tapeworms, have a pet passport and be on a course of medication for tapeworms 2 days before they enter. The UK is the strictest country I've encountered when it comes to travelling with pets so I use this as barometer. My point is, do your homework if you're bringing your furry friend, both about entry conditions and the local environment for your pet. For instance, in India, many domesticated dogs are attacked by street dogs. Educate yourself on your options and limitations but don't think because you have pets that travel is out of the question.

Kids

I also have a daughter who is about to turn 1. We have travelled to seven countries with her so far, with many more in the pipeline. The easiest way to travel with kids is in an RV. You don't have to worry about checking vast amounts of baggage or travelling with a stroller. You have unlimited freedom and can camp for free in many places. You can normally take the RV on a slow ship cheaper than the price of a plane ticket for 3 people.

A study by Cornell University found that we get more happiness from anticipating a travel experience in comparison to anticipating buying a new possession, so in that way, money can buy you happiness. If you invest in an RV, you can also turn it into a profit centre by renting it out on platforms like www.outdoorsy.com.

You don't necessarily have to fly to travel with kids, train, bus and RV's are better options. Kids become more adaptable and flexible when the world is their classroom. This is true at any age. but when kids immerse themselves in new places and engage with local cultures; this open-mindedness helps them in all aspects of their lives. For school-age children, you are limited to holiday dates, but with 12 weeks off a year, you can still find adventure together.

A spouse who doesn't want you to travel

A loving partner should always want what's best for you. Scientifically, travelling is proven to reduce stress. A study in 2000 study found that men and women who do not take a trip for several years are 30 per cent more likely to have a heart attack. It makes sense because when you travel you are more active; travellers often walk ten miles a day, sightseeing and soaking up new sights and smells.

Travelling also strengthens the 'openness' aspect of your personality and makes you less emotionally reactive to day-to-day changes, improving emotional stability. Sure, losing your baggage or almost missing a connecting flight can be panic-inducing, but, overall, the data supports that travelling is beneficial for you. Tell your partner about these studies, if they don't want a healthier, happier, more emotionally stable you, then it may be time to consider why you're investing your time with this person.

Another common issue is mismatched travel budgets. If you and your partner travel together and they force you to overspend with the 'we're on holiday/vacation!' appendage, here's a tip from one of our writers Kim:

'My husband and I were always having 'discussions' about money during our trips. I love bargains and he is the kind of traveller who's totally cool to be ripped off because he normally travels for business and has become used to spending corporate money. The compromise we reached is that he reads a shoestring or super cheap guide before the trip. Then when he wants to waste money, I say yes, but only in exchange for doing one budget item from the guide. It has worked wonders, lessened our 'discussions' and he now actually chooses cheaper destinations as he sees budgeting as a game.'

A job that keeps you at home

Our lives can feel constantly busy. Sometimes we may feel we are sinking beneath our workload. If you're close to or suffering a burnout the stress relief that comes from novelty and change in the form of new people, sights and experiences is the best remedy you could give to yourself.

If you're in a job that is hurting your health or well-being its time to reconsider why. It is often the case that you believe the work to be deeply rewarding, but if that reward leaves you ill, uninspired and fatigued, you can't help anyone. I learnt this the hard way when I worked for a charity whose mission I deeply resonated with. After 3 years of 70 hour work weeks, I'd lost hair, teeth, direction and, if I'm honest, faith in humanity. It took me 3 years to come back to the light and see that I chose a very stressful job that my body told me repeatedly it could not handle. Travel was a big part of forgiving myself. It helped me put old stories that held me back and probably sent me into this quagmire of self-abuse via work into perspective.

Sometimes we keep letting ourselves make excuses about why we're not travelling because we're scared of the unknown. In such cases, one of three things happens that forces a person from their nest:

- A traumatic event
- Completing a major milestone
- A sudden realisation or epiphany

Do yourself a favour, don't wait for any of those. Decide you want to travel, and book a flight. Our next section takes you through how to book the cheapest possible flight.

HOW TO FIND CHEAP FLIGHTS

"The use of travelling is to regulate imagination by reality, and instead of thinking how things may be, to see them as they are." Samuel Jackson

If you're working full-time you can save yourself a lot of money

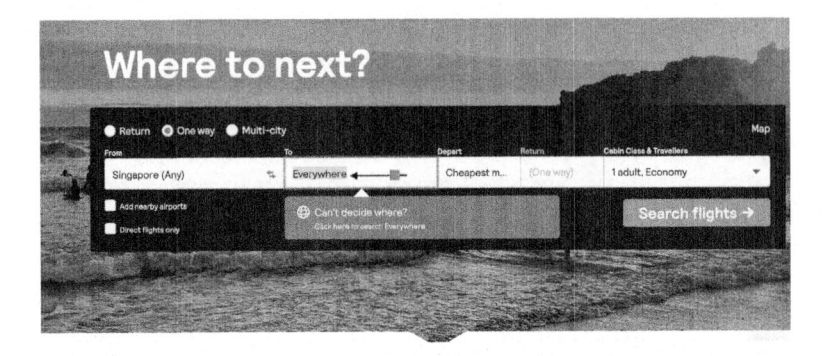

by requesting your time off from work starting in the middle of the week. Tuesdays and Wednesdays are the cheapest days to fly, you can save hundreds just by adjusting your time off.

The simplest secret to booking cheap flights is open parameters. Let's say you want to fly from Chicago to Paris. You need to enter USA to France, you may find flights from NYC to Paris for $70 and can take a cheap flight to NYC. Make sure you calculate full costs, including if you need airport accommodation and of course getting to and from airports, but in every instance open parameters will save you at least half the cost of the flight.

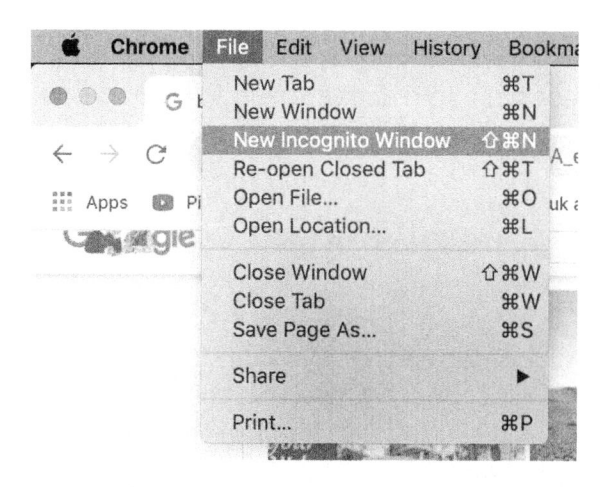

If you're not sure about where you want to go, use open parameters to show you the cheapest destinations from your city.
Use skyscanner.net - they include the low-cost airlines that others like Kayak leave out.

Open parameters can also show you the cheapest dates to fly. If you're flexible you can save up to 80% of the flight cost. Always check the weather at your destination before you book, sometimes a $400 flight will be $20, because its monsoon season. But hey, if you like the rain, why not?

ALWAYS USE A PRIVATE BROWSER TO BOOK FLIGHTS

Skyscanner and other sites track your IP address and put prices up and down based on what they determine your strength of conviction to buy. e.g if you've booked one-way and are looking for the return these sites will jack the prices up by in most cases 50%. Incognito browsing pays.

Use a VPN such as Hola to book your flight from your destination

Install Hola, change your destination to the country you are flying to. The location from which a ticket is booked can affect the price significantly as algorithms take into account local buying power.

Choose the right time to buy your ticket.

Choose the right time to buy your ticket, as purchasing tickets on a Sunday has been proven to be cheaper. If you can only book during the week, try to do it on a Tuesday.

Mistake fares

Email alerts from individual carriers are where you can find the best 'mistake fares". This is where a computer error has resulted in an airline offering the wrong fare. In my experience its best to sign up to individual carriers email lists but if you ARE lazy Secret Flying puts together a daily roster of mistake fares. Visit to see if there's any errors that can benefit you.

Fly late for cheaper prices.

Red-eye flights, the ones that leave later in the day, are typically cheaper and less crowded, so aim to book that flight if possible. You will also get through the airport much quicker at the end of the day, just make sure there's ground transport available for when you land. You don't want to save $50 on the airfare and spend it on a taxi to your accommodation.

Use this APP for same day flights

If you're plans are flexible, use 'Get The Flight Out' ( ) a fare tracker Hopper that shows you same-day deeply discounted flights. This is best for long-haul flights with major carriers. You can often find a British Airways round-trip from JFK Airport to Heathrow for $300. If you booked this in advance you'd pay at least double.

Take an empty water bottle with you

Airport prices on food and drinks are sky-high. It disgusts me to see some airports charging $10 for a bottle of water. ALWAYS take an empty water bottle with you. It's relatively unknown, but most airports have drinking water fountains past the security check. Just type in your airport name to to locate the fountain. Then once you've passed security (because they don't allow you to take 100ml or more of liquids) you can freely refill your bottle with water.

Round-the-World (RTW) Tickets

It is always cheaper to book your flights using a DIY approach. First, you may decide you want to stay longer in one country, and a RTW will charge you a hefty fee for changing your flight. Secondly, it all depends on where and when you travel and as we have discussed, there are many ways to ensure you pay way less than $1,500 for a year of flights. If you're travelling long-haul, the best strategy is to buy a return ticket, say New York to Bangkok and then take cheap flights or transport around Asia and even to Australia and beyond.

Frequent Flyer Memberships

A frequent-flyer program (FFP) is a loyalty program offered by an airline. They are designed to encourage airline customers to fly more to accumulate points (also called miles, kilometres, or segments) which can be redeemed for air travel or other rewards.

You can sign up with any FFP program for free. There are three major airline alliances in the world: Oneworld, SkyTeam and Star Alliance. I am with One World https://www.oneworld.com/members because the points can be accrued and used for most flights.

The best return on your points is to use them for international business or first class flights with lie-flat seats. You would need 3 times more miles compared to an economy flight, but if you paid cash, you'd pay 5 - 10 times more than the cost of the economy flight, so it really pays to use your points only for upgrades. The worst value for your miles is to buy an economy seat or worse, a gift from the airlines gift-shop.

Sign up for a family/household account to pool miles together. If you share a common address you can claim the miles with most airlines. You can use [AwardWallet](#) to keep track of your miles. Remember that they only last for 2 years, so use them before they expire.

Pack like a Pro

"He who would travel happily must travel light." – Antoine de St. Exupery 59.

Travel as lightly as you can. We always need less than we think. You will be very grateful that you have a light pack when changing trains, travelling through the airport, catching a bus, walking to your accommodation, or climbing stairs.

Make a list of what you will wear for 7 days and take only those clothes. You can easily wash your things while you're travelling if you stay in an Airbnb with a washing machine or visit a local laundrette. Roll your clothes for maximum space usage and fewer wrinkles. If you feel really nervous about travelling with such few things make sure you have a dressier outfit, a little black dress for women is always valuable, a shirt for men. Then pack shorts, long pair of pants, loose tops and a hoodie to snuggle in. Remind yourself that a lack of clothing options is an opportunity to find bargain new outfits in thrift stores. You can either sell these on eBay after you've worn them or post them home to yourself. You'll feel less stressed, as you don't have to look after or feel weighed down by excess baggage. Here are three things to remember when packing:

- Co-ordinate colours - make sure everything you bring can be worn together.
- Be happy to do laundry - fresh clothes when you're travelling feels very luxurious.
- Take liquid minis no bigger than 60ml. Liquid is heavy and you simply don't need to carry so much at one time.

Checks to Avoid Fees

Always have 6 months validity on your passport

To enter most countries you need 6 months from the day you land. Factor in different time zones around the world if your passport is on the edge. Airport security will stop you from boarding your flight at the airport if your passport has 5 months and 29 days left.

Google Your Flight Number before you leave for the airport

Easily find out where your plane is from anywhere. Confirm the status of your flight before you leave for the airport with flightaware.com. This can save you long unnecessary wait times.

Check-in online

The founder, Ryan O'Leary of budget airline RyanAir famously said: "We think they should pay €60 for [failing to check-in on-line] being so stupid.". Always check-in online, even for international flights. Cheaper international carriers like Scoot will charge you at the airport to check-in.

Checking Bags

Never, ever check a bag if you possibly can avoid it. It is always cheaper to put heavier items on a ship, rather than take them on a flight with you. Find the best prices for shipping at https://www.parcelmonkey.com/delivery-services/shipping-heavy-items

Use a fragile sticker

Put a 'Fragile' sticker on anything you check to ensure that it's handled better as it goes through security. It'll also be one of the first bags released after the flight, getting you out of the airport quicker.

If you do check your bag, photograph it

Take a photo of your bag before you check it. This will speed up the paperwork if it is damaged or lost.

Relaxing at the airport

The best way to relax at the airport is in a lounge where they provide free food, drinks, comfortable chairs, luxurious amenities (many have showers) and if you're lucky a peaceful ambience. If you're there for a longer time look for Airport Cubicles, sleep pods which charge by the hour.

You can use your FFP Card (Frequent Flyer Memberships) to get into select lounges for free. Check your eligibility before you pay.

If you're travelling a lot I'd recommend to Invest in a Priority Pass for the airport.
It includes 850-plus airport lounges around the world. The cost is $99 for the year and $27 per lounge visit or you can pay $399 for the year all inclusive.

If you need a lounge pass for a one-off day, you can get a Day Pass. Buy it online for a discount, it always works out cheaper than buying at the airport. Use

Lounges are also great if you're travelling with kids, as they're normally free for kids and will definitely cost you less than snacks for your little ones. The rule is that kids should be seen and not heard, so consider this before taking an overly excited child who wants to run around, or you might be asked to leave even after you've paid.

Money: How to make it, spend it and save it while travelling

How to earn money WHILE travelling

"Twenty years from now you will be more disappointed by the things you didn't do than by the ones you did do. So throw off the bowlines. Sail away from the safe harbour." - H. Jackson Brown

Digital nomads receive a lot of hype. Put simply they are "professionals who work online and therefore don't need to tie themselves to one particular office, city, or even country."

The first step in becoming a digital nomad, earning money while travelling is knowing what you can offer. Your market is the whole world. So, what product or service would you like to offer that they would pay for? Take some time to think about this. In German, they say you should do whatever comes easily to your hand. For example, I've always loved finding bargains, it comes very easily for me. Yet I studied Law and Finance at University, which definitely did not come easy. It's no shock that it didn't transpire into a career. And served more as a lesson in not following my ego.

There are thousands of possibilities to generate income while travelling; offering services like tutorial, coaching, writing service pr blogging. Most travellers I meet try their hand at blogging and earning from the advertisements. This is great if you have some savings, but if you need to earn straight away to travel, this should be on the back burner, as it takes time to establish. Still if this comes easily to you, do it!

You want to make good money fast. Ask yourself, what is it that you are good at and how can you deliver maximum value to other people? Here are some ideas if you're totally dumfounded:

1. Teaching English online - you will need a private room for this. Be aware that if you're from the USA and the country you want to work in requires a federal-level background check, it

may take months, so apply early. Opportunities are on: t.vipkid.com.cn, abc360.com, italki.com, verbalplanet.com and verbling.com. You can expect to earn $20 an hour.
2. Work in a hostel. Normally you'll get some cash and free accommodation.
3. Fruit picking. I picked Bananas in Tully Australia for $20 an hour. The jobs are menial but can be quite meditative. Look on WWOOF.org for organic farm work.
4. fiverr.com - offer a small service, like making a video template and changing the content for each buyer.
5. Do freelance work online: marketing, finance, writing, App creation, graphic designer, UX or UI designer, SEO optimizer / expert. Create a profile on upwork.com - you need to put in a lot of work to make this successful, but if you have a unique skill like coding, or marketing it can be very lucrative.
6. Make a udemy.com course. Can you offer a course in something people will pay for? e.g. stock trading, knitting or marketing.
7. Use skype to deliver all manner of services: language lessons, therapy, coaching etc. Google for what you could offer. Most specialisms have a platform you can use to find clients and they will take a cut of your earnings/ require a fee.
8. You could work on luxury yachts in the med. Its hard work, but you can save money - DesperateSailors.com
9. Become an Airbnb experience host - but this requires you to know one place and stay there for a time. And you will need a work visa for that country.
10. Work on a cruise ship. This isn't a digital nomad job but it will help you travel and save at the same time.
11. Rent your place out on airbnb while you travel and get a cleaner to manage it. The easiest solution if you own or have a long-term rent contract.

How to spend money

Budget travel hacking begins with a strategy to spend without fees. Your individual strategy depends greatly on the country you legally reside in as to what cards are available. Happily there are some fin-tech solutions which can save you thousands and are widely available globally. I will address those first:

N26
N26 is a 10-year old digital bank. I have been using them for over 6 years. The key advantage is fee-free card transactions abroad. They have a very elegant app, where you can check your timeline for all transactions listed in realtime or manage your in-app security anywhere. The card you receive is a Mastercard so you can use it everywhere. If you lose the card, you don't have to call anyone, just open the app and swipe 'lock card'. It puts your purchases into a graph automatically so you can see what you spend on. You can open an account from abroad entirely online, all you need is your passport and a camera

Revolut
Revolut is a multi-currency account that allows you to hold and exchange 29 currencies and spend fee-free abroad. It's a UK based neobank, but accepts customers from all over the world.

TransferWise debit card
If you're going to be in one place for a long time the The TransferWise debit card is like having your travel money on a card – it lets you spend money at the real exchange rate.

Monzo
Monzo is good if your UK based. They offer a fee-free UK account. Fee-free international money transfers and fee-free spending abroad.

The downside

The cards above are debit cards, meaning you need to have money in those accounts to spend it. This comes with one big downside: safety. Credit card issuers' have "zero liability" meaning you're not liable for unauthorised charges. All of the cards listed above do provide cover for unauthorised charges but times vary greatly in how quickly you'd get your money back if it were stolen.

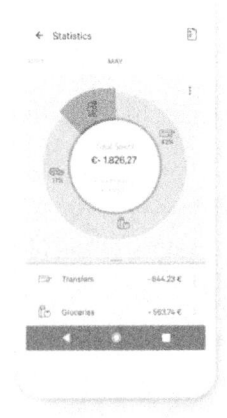

The best option is to check in your country to see which credit cards are the best for travelling and set up monthly payments to repay the whole amount so you don't pay unnecessary interest. In the USA, Schwab[1] regularly ranks at the top for travel credit cards. Credit cards are always the safer option when abroad simply because you get your money back faster if its stolen and if you're renting cars, most will give you free insurance when you book the car rental using the card, saving you money.

---

[1] Charles Schwab High Yield Checking accounts refund every single ATM fee worldwide, require no minimum balance and have no monthly fee.

Always withdraw money; never exchange.

Money exchanges whether they be on the streets or in the airports will NEVER give you a good exchange rate. Do not bring bundles of cash. Instead withdraw local currency from the ATM as needed and try to use only free ATM's. Many in airports charge you a fee to withdraw cash. Look for bigger ATM's attached to banks to avoid this.

Recap:

- Take cash from local, non-charging ATMs for the best rates.
- Never change at airport exchange desks unless you absolutely have to, then just change just enough to be able get to a bank ATM.
- Bring a spare credit card for emergencies.
- Split cash in various places on your person (pockets, shoes) and in your luggage. Its never sensible to keep your cash or cards all in one place.
- In higher risk areas, use a money belt under your clothes or put $50 in your shoe or bra.

How to save money while travelling

Saving money while travelling sounds like an oxymoron, but it can be done with little to no effort. Einstein is credited as saying, "Compound interest is the eighth wonder of the world." If you saved and invested $100 today, in 20 years it would be $2,000 thanks to the power of compound interest. It makes sense then to save your money, invest and make even more money.

The Acorns app is a simple system for this. It rounds up your credit card purchases and puts the rest into a savings account. So if you pay for a coffee and its $3.01, you'll save 0.99 cents. You won't even notice you're saving by using this app:

Here are some more generic ways you can always save money while travelling:

Device Safety
Having your phone, iPad or laptop stolen is one BIG and annoying way you can lose money traveling. The simple solution is to use apps to track your devices. Some OSes have this feature built-in. Prey will try your smartphones or laptops (preyproject.com).

Book New Airbnb's
When you take a risk on a new Airbnb listing, you save money. Just make sure the hosts profile is at least 3 years old and has reviews.

If you end up in an overcrowded city

The website   is like Airbnb for camping in people's garden and is a great way to save money if you end up in a city during a big event.

Look out for free classes
Lots of hostels offer free classes for guests. If you're planning to stay in a hostel, check out what classes your hostel offers. I have learnt languages, cooking techniques, dance styles, drawing and all manner of things for free by taking advantage of free classes at hostels.

Get a student discount card
If you're studying buy an ISIC card - International Student Identity Card. It is internationally recognised, valid in 133 countries and offers more than 150,000 discounts!

Instal
Maps me is extremely good for travelling without data. It's like offline google maps without the huge download size.

Always buy travel insurance
Don't travel without travel insurance. It is a small cost to pay compared with what could be a huge medical bill.

How to ensure your travel insurance covers you for COVID-19

Many insurers stopped selling travel insurance after the start of the pandemic, some have returned with some form of 'COVID-19 cover'. MoneySupermarket.com is updating a list of insurers who cover you for varying degrees of pandemic-related travel disruption. Check on their website before buying a policy to avoid having to wade through the fine print - much of which is not written in plain English and may contain degrees of pandemic coverage such as they will pay your medical expenses but not your flight home. Book hotels and flights with a credit card that cover pandemic-related travel expenses for an added level of security.

REMEMBER if you travel to a country your government is currently advising against travel to for your planned dates, then it's likely that you won't be covered at all.

Travel Apps That'll Make Budget Travel Easier

Travel apps are useful for booking and managing travel logistics. They have one fatal downside, they can track you in the app and keep prices up. If you face this, access the site from an incognito browser tab.

Here are the best apps and what they can do for you:

- Best For flight Fare-Watching: Hopper.
- Best for booking flights: Skyscanner
- Best for timing airport arrivals: FlightAware - check on delays, cancellations and gate changes.
- Best for overcoming a fear of flying: SkyGuru - turbulence forecasts for the route you're flying.
- Best for sharing your location: TripWhistle - text or send your GPS coordinates or location easily.
- Best for splitting expenses among co-travellers: Splittr, Trip Splitter, Venmo or Splitwise.

We have covered the best apps and websites for Florence in the section above called useful websites.

How NOT to be ripped off

"One of the great things about travel is that you find out how many good, kind people there are."
— Edith Wharton

The quote above may seem ill placed in a chapter entitled how not to be ripped off, but I included it to remind you that the vast majority of people do not want to rip you off. In fact, scammers are normally limited to three situations:

1. Around heavily visited attractions - these places are targeted purposively due to sheer footfall. Many criminals believe ripping people off is simply a numbers game.
2. In cities or countries with low-salaries or communist ideologies. If they can't make money in the country, they seek to scam foreigners. If you have travelled to India, Morocco or Cuba you will have observed this phenomenon.
3. When you are stuck and the person helping you knows you have limited options.

Scammers know that most people will avoid confrontation. Don't feel bad about utterly ignoring someone and saying no. Here are six strategies to avoid being ripped off:

1. **Never ever agree to pay as much as you want. Always decide on a price before.**
Whoever you're dealing with is trained to tell you, they are uninterested in money. This is a trap. If you let people do this they will ask for MUCH MORE money at the end, and because you have used there service, you will feel obliged to pay. This is a con-man's trick and nothing more.

2. **Pack light**
You can move faster and easier. If you take heavy luggage you will end up taking taxi's which are comparatively very costly over time.

3. NEVER use the airport taxi service. Plan to use public transport before you reach the airport.

4. Don't buy a sim card from the airport. Buy from the local supermarkets it will cost 50% less.

5. Eat at local restaurants serving regional food
Food defines culture. Exploring all delights available to the palate doesn't need to cost huge sums.

6. Ask the locals what something should cost, and try not to pay over that.

7. If you find yourself with limited options. e.g. your taxi dumps you on the side of the road because you refuse to pay more (common in India and parts of South America) don't act desperate and negotiate as if you have other options or you will be extorted.

8. Don't blindly rely on social media

Let's say you post in a Facebook group that you want tips for travelling to The Maldives. A lot of the comments you will receive come from guides, hosts and restaurants doing their own promotion. It's estimated that 50% or more of Facebook's current monthly active users are fake[2]. And what's worse, a recent study found Social media platforms leave 95% of reported fake accounts up[3]. These accounts are the digital versions of the men who hang around the Grand Palace in Bangkok telling tourists its closed, to divert you to

---

[2]

[3]

shops where they will receive a commission for bringing you.

It can also be the case that genuine comments come from people who have totally different interests, beliefs and yes, budgets to yours. Make your experience your own and don't believe every comment you read.

Bottom line: use caution when accepting recommendations on social media and always fact-check with your own research.

Small tweaks on the road add up to big differences in your bank balance

Take advantage of other hotel's amenities

If you fancy a swim but you're nowhere near the ocean, try the nearest hotel with a pool. As long as you buy a drink, the hotel staff will likely grant you access.

Fill up your mini bar for free.

Fill up your mini bar for free by storing things from the breakfast bar or grocery shop in your mini bar to give you a greater selection of drinks and food without the hefty price tag.

Save yourself some ironing

Use the steam from the shower to get rid of wrinkles in clothing. If something is creased, leave it trapped with the steam in the bathroom overnight for even better results.

See somewhere else for free

Opt for long stopovers, allowing you to experience another city without spending much money.

Wear your heaviest clothes

on the plane to save weight in your pack, allowing you to bring more with you. Big coats can then be used as pillows to make your flight more comfortable.

Don't get lost while you're away.

Find where you want to go using Google Maps, then type 'OK Maps' into the search bar to store this information for offline viewing.

Use car renting services

Share Now or Car2Go allow you to hire a car for 2 hours for $25 in a lot of Europe.

Share Rides

Use sites like blablacar.com to find others who are driving in your direction. It can be 80% cheaper than normal transport. Just check the drivers reviews.

Use free gym passes

Get a free gym day pass by googling the name of a local gym and free day pass.

When asked by people providing you a service where you are from..

If there's no price list for the service you are asking for, when asked where you are from, Say you are from a lesser-known poorer country. I normally say Macedonia, and if they don't know where it is, add it's a poor country. If you say UK, USA, the majority of Europe bar the well-known poorer countries taxi drivers, tour operators etc will match the price to what they think you pay at home.

Set-up a New Uber/ other car hailing app account for discounts

By googling you can find offers with $50 free for new users in most cities for Uber/ Lyft/ Bolt and alike. Just set up a new gmail.com email account to take advantage.

Where and How to Make Friends

"People don't take trips, trips take people." – John Steinbeck

Become popular at the airport

Want to become popular at the airport? Pack a power bar with multiple outlets and just see how many friends you can make. It's amazing how many people forget their chargers, or who packed them in the luggage that they checked in.

Stay in Hostels

First of all, Hostels don't have to be shared dorms, and they cater to a much wider demographic than is assumed. Hostels are a better environment for meeting people than hotels, and more importantly they tended to open up excursion opportunities that further opened up that opportunity.

Or take up a hobby

If hostels are a definite no-no for you; find an interest. Take up a hobby where you will meet people. I've dived for years and the nature of diving is you're always paired up with a dive buddy. I met a lot of interesting people that way.

When unpleasantries come your way...

We all have our good and bad days travelling, and on a bad day you can feel like just taking a flight home. Here are some ways to overcome common travel problems:

Anxiety when flying

It has been over 40 years since a plane has been brought down by turbulence. Repeat that number to yourself: 40 years! Planes are built to withstand lighting strikes, extreme storms and ultimately can adjust course to get out of their way. Landing and take off are when the most accidents happen, but you have statistically three times the chance of winning a huge jackpot lottery, then you do of dying in a plane crash.

If you feel afraid on the flight focus on your breathing saying the word 'smooth' over and over until the flight is smooth. Always check the airline safety record on airlinerating.com I was surprised to learn Ryanair and Easyjet as much less safe than Wizz Air according to those ratings because they sell similarly priced flights. If there is extreme turbulence, I feel much better knowing I'm in a 7 star safety plane.

Wanting to sleep instead of seeing new places

This is a common problem. Just relax, there's little point doing fun things when you feel tired. Factor in jet-lag to your travel plans. When you're rested and alert you'll enjoy your new temporary home much more. Many people hate the first week of a long-trip because of jet-lag and often blame this on their first destination, but its rarely true. Ask travellers who 'hate' a particular place and you will see, that very often they either had jet-lag or an unpleasant journey there.

Going over budget

Come back from a trip to a monster credit card bill? Hopefully this guide has prevented you from returning to an unwanted bill. Of course, there are costs that can creep up and this is a reminder about how to prevent them making their way on to your credit card bill:

- To and from the airport. Solution: leave adequate time and take the cheapest method - book before.
- Baggage. Solution: take hand luggage and post things you might need to yourself.
- Eating out. Solution: go to cheap eats places and suggest those to friends.
- Parking. Solution: use apps to find free parking
- Tipping. Solution Leave a modest tip and tell the server you will write them a nice review.
- Souvenirs. Solution: fridge magnets only.
- Giving to the poor. (This one still gets me, but if you're giving away $10 a day - it adds up) Solution: volunteer your time instead and recognise that in tourist destinations many beggars are run by organised crime gangs.

Price v Comfort

I love traveling, I don't love struggling. I like decent accommodation, being able to eat properly and see places and enjoy. I am never in the mood for low cost airlines or crappy transfers so here's what I do to save money.

- Avoid organised tours unless you are going to a place where safety is a real issue. They are expensive and constrain your wanderlust to typical things. I only recommend them in Algeria, Iran and Papua New Guinea - where language and gender views pose serious problems all cured by a reputable tour organiser.
- Eat what the locals do.
- Cook in your airbnb/ hostel where restaurants are expensive.
- Shop at local markets.
- Spend time choosing your flight, and check the operator on <u>arilineratings.com</u>
- Mix up hostels and Airbnbs. Hostels for meeting people, Airbnb for relaxing and feeling 'at home'.

Not knowing where free toilets are

Use Toilet Finder - <u>https://play.google.com/store/apps/details?id=com.bto.toilet&hl=en</u>

Your airbnb is awful

Airbnb customer service is notoriously bad. Help yourself out. Try to sort things out with the host, but if you can't, take photos of everything e.g bed, bathroom, mess, doors, contact them within 24 hours. Tell them you had to leave and pay for new accommodation. Ask politely for a full refund including booking fees. With photographic evidence and your new accommodation receipt, they can't refuse.

The airline loses your bag

Go to the Luggage desk before leaving the airport and report the bag missing.
Most airlines will give you an overnight bag, ask where your staying and return the bag to you within three days. Its extremely rare for them to completely lose it due to technological innovation, but if that happens you should submit an insurance claim after the

three days is up, including receipts for everything your had to buy in the interim.

Your travel companion lets you down.

Whether it's a breakup or a friend cancelling, it sucks and can ramp up costs. The easiest solution to finding a new travel companion is to go to a well-reviewed hostel and find someone you want to travel with. You should spend at least three days getting to know this person before you suggest travelling together. Finding someone in person is always better than finding someone online, because you can get a better idea of whether you will have a smooth journey together. Travel can make or break friendships.

Culture shock

I had one of the strongest culture shocks while spending 6 months in Japan. It was overwhelming how much I had to prepare when I went outside of the door (googling words and sentences what to use, where to go, which station and train line to use, what is this food called in Japanese and how does its look etc.). I was so tired constantly but in the end I just let go and went with my extremely bad Japanese. If you feel culture shocked its because your brain is referencing your surroundings to what you know. Stop comparing, have Google translate downloaded and relax.

Your Car rental insurance is crazy expensive

I always use carrentals.com and book with a credit card. Most credit cards will give you free insurance for the car, so you don't need to pay the extra.

You're sick

First off ALWAYS, purchase travel insurance. Including emergency transport up to $500k even to back home, which is usually less than $10 additional. I use https://www.comparethemarket.com/travel-insurance/ to find the best days. If I am sick I normally check into a hotel with room service and ride it out.

Make a Medication Travel Kit

Take travel sized medications with you:

- Antidiarrheal medication (for example, bismuth subsalicylate, loperamide)
- Medicine for pain or fever (such as acetaminophen, aspirin, or ibuprofen)
- Throat Lozenges

Save yourself from most travel related hassles

- Do not make jokes with immigration and customs staff. A misunderstanding can lead to HUGE fines.

- Book the most direct flight you can find, nonstop if possible.

- Carry a US$50 bill for emergency cash. I have entered a country and all ATM and credit card systems were down. US$ can be exchanged nearly anywhere in the world and is useful in extreme situations, but where possible don't exchange, as you will lose money.

- Check, and recheck, required visas and such BEFORE the day of your trip. Some countries, for instance, require a ticket out of the country in order to enter. Others, like the

US and Australia, require electronic authorisation in advance.

- Airport security is asinine and inconsistent around the world. Keep this in mind when connecting flights. Always leave at least 2 hours for international connections or international to domestic. In London Stansted for example, they force you to buy one of their plastic bags, and remove your liquids from your own plastic bag…. just to make money from you. And this adds to the time it will take to get through security so lines are long.

- Wiki travel is perfect to use for a lay of the land.

- Expensive luggage rarely lasts longer than cheap luggage, in my experience. Fancy leather bags are toast with air travel.
-

Food

- When it comes to food, eat in local restaurants, not tourist-geared joints. Any place with the menu in three or more languages is going to be overpriced.
- Take a spork - a knife, spoon and fork all in one.

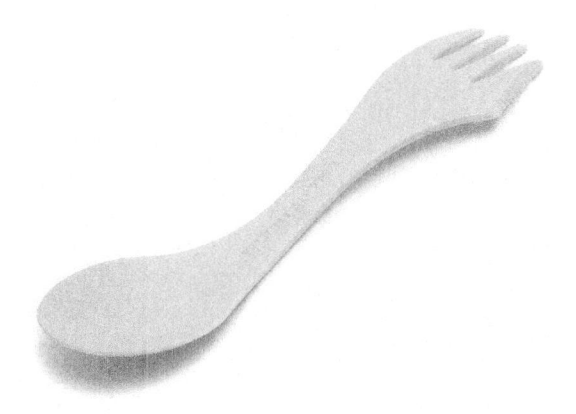

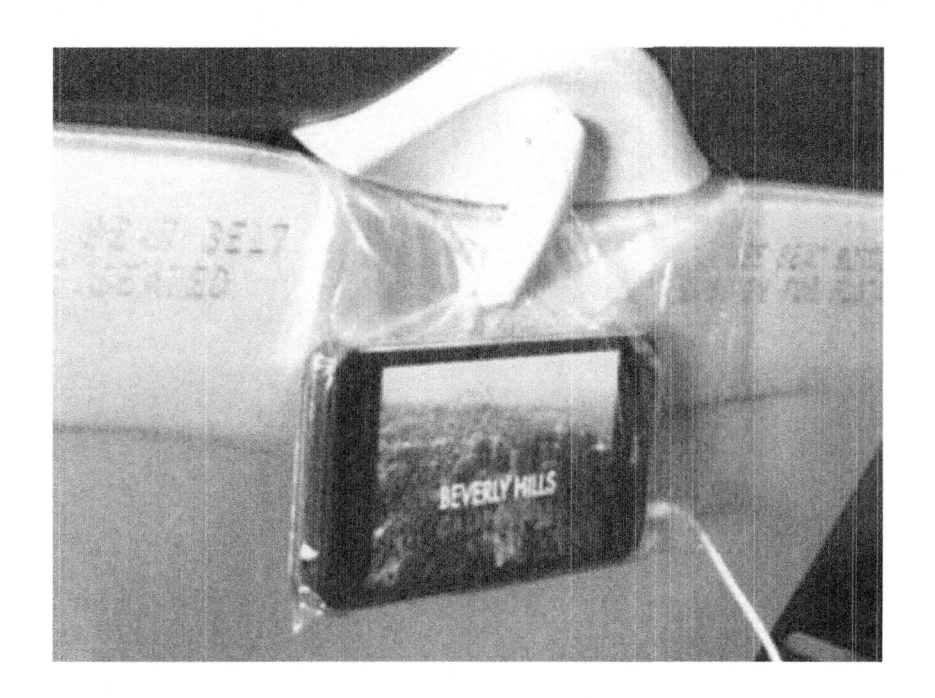

Water Bottle

Take a water bottle with a filter. We love these ones from Water to Go.
Empty it before airport security and separate the bottle and filter as some airport people will try and claim it has liquids…

Bug Sprays

If you're heading somewhere tropical spray your clothes with Permethrin before you travel. It lasts 40 washes and saves space in your bag. A 'Bite Away' zapper can be used after the bite to totally erase it. It cuts down on the itching and erases the bite from your skin.

Order free mini's

Don't buy those expensive travel sized toiletries, order travel sized freebies online. This gives you the opportunity to try brands you've never used before, and who knows, you might even find your new favourite soap.

Take a waterproof bag

If you're travelling alone you can swim without worrying about your phone, wallet and passport laying on the beach. You can also use it as a source of entertainment on those ultra budget flights.

Make a private entertainment centre anywhere

Always take an eye-mask, earplugs, a scarf and a kindle reader - so you can sleep and entertain yourself anywhere!

The best Travel Gadgets

The door alarm

If you're nervous and staying in private rooms or airbnbs take a door alarm. For those times when you just don't feel safe, it can help you fall asleep. You can get tiny ones for less than $10 from Amazon:

Smart Blanket

Amazon sells a 6 in 1 heating blanket that is very useful for cold plane or bus trips. Its great if you have poor circulation as it becomes a detachable Foot Warmer: Amazon http://amzn.to/2hTYlOP I paid $49.00.

The coat that becomes a tent

https://www.adiff.com/products/tent-jacket. This is great if you're going to be doing a lot of camping.

Clever Tank Top with Secret Pockets

Keep your valuables safe in this top. Perfect for all climates.

on Amazon for $39.90

Optical Camera Lens for Smartphones and Tablets
Leave your bulky camera at home. Turn your device into a high-performance camera. Buy on Amazon for $9.95

Travel-sized Wireless Router with USB Media Storage

Convert any wired network to a wireless network. Buy on Amazon for $17.99

Buy a Scrubba Bag to wash your clothes on the go
Or a cheaper imitable. You can wash your clothes on the go.

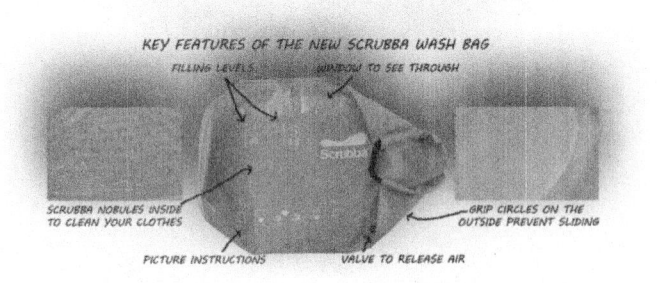

![Scrubba Wash Bag with labeled features: KEY FEATURES OF THE NEW SCRUBBA WASH BAG — FILLING LEVELS, WINDOW TO SEE THROUGH, SCRUBBA NOBULES INSIDE TO CLEAN YOUR CLOTHES, GRIP CIRCLES ON THE OUTSIDE PREVENT SLIDING, PICTURE INSTRUCTIONS, VALVE TO RELEASE AIR]

Hacks for Families

Rent an Airbnb apartment so you can cook

Apartments are much better for families, as you have all the amenities you'd have at home. They are normally cheaper per person too. We are the first travel guide publisher to include Airbnb's in our recommendations if you think any of these need updating you can email me at philgtang@gmail.com

Shop at local markets

Eat seasonal products and local products. Get closer to the local market and observe the prices and the offer. What you can find more easily, will be the cheapest

Take Free Tours

Download free podcast tours of the destination you are visiting. The podcast will tell you where to start, where to go, and what to look for. Often you can find multiple podcast tours of the same place. Listen to all of them if you like, each one will tell you a little something new.

Pack Extra Ear Phones

If you go on a museum tour, they often have audio guides. Instead of having to rent one for each person, take some extra earphones. Most audio tour devices have a place to plug in a second set.

Buy Souvenirs Ahead of Time

If you are buying souvenirs, something touristy, you are paying a premium price. By ordering the exact same product online from sites like Aliexpress.com, you save a lot of money and hassle. You can have them shipped to your home address so you don't have to carry them around, but still have something to give friends and family when you return.

Use Cheap Transportation

Do as the locals do, including checking out weekly passes.

Carry Reusable Water Bottles

Spending money on water and other beverages can quickly add up. Instead of paying for drinks, take some refillable water bottles.

Combine Attractions

Many major cities offer ticket bundles where one price gets you into 5 or 6 popular attractions. You will need to plan ahead of time to decide what things you plan to do on vacation and see if they are selling these activities together.

Pack Snacks

Granola bars, apples, baby carrots, bananas, cheese crackers, juice boxes, pretzels, fruit snacks, apple sauce, grapes, and veggie chips.

Stick to Carry-On Bags

Do not pay to check a large bag. Even a small child can pull a carry-on.

Visit free art galleries and museums

Just google the name + free days.

Eat Street Food

There's a lot of unnecessary fear around this. You can watch the food prepared. Go for the stands that have a steady queue.

Travel Gadgets for Families

Dropcam

Are what-if scenarios playing out in your head? Then you need Dropcam.

'Dropcam HD Internet Wi-Fi Video Monitoring Cameras help you watch what you love from anywhere. In less than a minute, you'll have it setup and securely streaming video to you over your home Wi-Fi. Watch what you love while away with Dropcam HD.'

Approximate Price: $139

Kelty-Child-Carrier

Voted as one of the best hiking essentials if you're traveling with kids and can carry a child up to 18kg.

Jetkids Bedbox

No more giving up your own personal space on the plane with this suitcase that becomes a bed.

Safety

"If you think adventure is dangerous, try routine. It's lethal." – Paulo Coelho

Backpacker murdered is a media headline that leads people to think traveling is more dangerous than it is. The media sensationalise the rare murders and deaths of backpackers and travellers. The actual chances of you dying abroad are extremely extremely low.

Let's take the USA as an example. In 2018, 724 Americans **died** from unnatural causes, 167 died from car accidents, while the majority of the other deaths resulted from drownings, suicides, and non-vehicular accidents. Contrast this with the 15,000 murders in the US in 2018, and travelling abroad looks much safer than staying at home.

There are many thing you can to keep yourself save. Here are out tips.

1. Always check fco.co.uk before travelling. NEVER RELY on websites or books. Things are changing constantly and the FCO's (UK's foreign office) advice is always UP TO DATE (hourly) and extremely conservative.
2. Check your mindset. I've travelled alone to over 180 countries and the main thing I learnt is if you walk around scared, or anticipating you're going to be pickpocketed, your constant fear will attract bad energy. Murders or attacks on travellers are the mainstay of media, not reality, especially in countries familiar with travellers. The only place I had cause to genuinely fear for my life was Papa New Guinea - where nothing actually happened to me only my own panic over culture shock.

There are many things you can do to stop yourself being victim to the two main problems when travelling: theft or being scammed.

I will address theft first. Here are my top tips:

- Stay alert while you're out and always have an exit strategy.
- Keep your money in a few different places on your person and your passport somewhere it can't be grabbed.
- Take a photo of your passport on your phone incase. If you do lose it, google for your embassy, you can usually get a temporary pretty fast.
- Google safety tips for traveling in your country to help yourself out and memorise the emergency number.
- At hostels keep your large bag in the room far under the bed/out of the way with a lock on the zipper.
- On buses/trains I would even lock my bag to the luggage rack.
- Get a personal keychain alarm. The sound will scare anyone away.
- Don't wear any jewellery. A man attempted to rob a friend of her engagement ring in Bogota, Colombia, and in hindsight I wished I'd told her to leave it at home/wear it on a hidden necklace, as the chaos it created was avoidable.
- Don't turn your back to traffic while you use your phone.
- When traveling in the tuktuk sit in the middle and keep your bag secure. Wear sunglasses as dust can easily get in your eyes.
- Don't let anyone give you flowers, bracelets, or any type of trinket, even if they insist it's for free and compliment you like crazy.
- Don't let strangers know that you are alone - unless they are travel friends ;-)
- Lastly, and most importantly -Trust your gut! If it doesn't feel right, it isn't.

Hilarious Travel Stories

I have compiled these short stories from fellow travellers to pick you up when you're feeling down. Life on the road isn't always easy and we've all had those days when we want to stay in bed and forget the world exists. Laughter is the best way I know to shake those feelings. All people who have shared these stories wanted to remain anonymous. After reading them I think you'll understand why...

I mentioned my wife earlier, so its only fair she be the first story. Don't worry she has given me permission to share.

A marriage up the wall

'Delhi belly got me on the third day into the trip to India. I was vomiting so much that I couldn't keep even water down so I went to a health clinic for tourists. Whilst I was there I was asked to poop into a jar and happily put on a drip.

The doctor attending me was mid to late 40's and very creepy. I decided I'd leave the clinic after my 4th bag of fluids because I felt better and was weirded out by the intense stares of my doctor. As I was paying the bill, the doctor came over, dropped to one knee and asked me to marry him at the desk. I stuttered in shock that I was already was married. He was holding a jar of my poo in his hand, stood and then chucked it at the wall. The jar broke open and my watery specimen was literally smeared across the wall as he trudged off. The woman serving me bobbed her head from side to side as if we were discussing the weather and said 'its not personal madam, you look like his last wife.'

Glass shame

'I was in Nashville airport in the smoking room. I heard my name being called for my flight so I rushed out but instead of rushing through the door, I walked smack into the glass. When I opened the door the entire departure lounge was roaring with laughter.'

The Dashing Date

'I had a date with a fellow Brit in Medellin. I went to the bathroom and when I came back, I asked him if he had paid the bill and he replied 'yes'. We were going down some stairs when he suddenly shouted at me to run. Yes, the restaurant staff were running after us because he hadn't paid.'

A fear of farting in hostels

'When I arrived to stay in my first ever hostel in London, I realised I had an intense fear
farting in my sleep. I literally gave myself such bad constipation I had to go to hospital. It turns out an enema is worse than hostel farting.'

What a boob
I fell on the Tube in London getting into a carriage. Unfortunately I managed to grab a woman's boob on the way to the floor. I was so mortified I walked everywhere else during the trip.'

Cementing a few laughs

'I was walking on the streets in Singapore when they were fixing the roads. I somehow stepped in fresh cement. I only noticed when my feet became so heavy I thought I had twisted my ankle. The cement got so hard, I had to take my shoes off as I couldn't pick up my feet. Locals were very clearly entertained as I walked back to my accommodation in my sponge bob squarepants socks.

If you've got a hilarious travel story you'd love to share, email me at   . All identifying details will be removed.

How I got hooked on budget travelling

'We're on holiday' is what my dad used to say to justify getting us in so much debt we lost our home and all our things when I was 11. We moved from the suburban bliss of Hemel Hempstead to a run down council estate in inner-city London, near my dad's new job as a refuge collector, a fancy word for dustbin man. I lost all my school friends while watching my dad go through a nervous breakdown.

My dad loved walking up a hotel lobby desk without a care in the world. So much so, that he booked overpriced holidays on credit cards. A lot of holidays. As it turned out we couldn't afford any of them. In the end, my dad had no choice but to declare bankruptcy. When my mum realised he'd racked up so much debt our family unit dissolved. A neat and perhaps as painless a summary of events that lead me to my life's passion: budget travel that doesn't compromise on fun, safety or comfort.

I started travelling full-time at the age of 18. I wrote the first Super Cheap Insider guide for friends visiting Norway - which I did for a month on less than $250. When sales reached 10,000 I decided to form the Super Cheap Insider Guides company. As I know from first-hand experience debt can be a noose around our necks, and saying 'oh come on, we're on vacation' isn't a get out of jail free card.

Before I embarked upon writing Super Cheap Insider guides many, many people told me that my dream was impossible, travelling on a budget could never be comfortable. I hope this guide has proved to you what I have known for a long-time: budget travel can feel luxurious when you know and use the insider hacks.

And apologies, if I depressed you with my tale of woe. My dad is now happily remarried and works as a chef in London at a fancy hotel - the kind he used to take us to!

A final word...

There's a simple system you can use to think about budget travel. In life we can choose two of the following: cheap, fast or quality. So if you want it Cheap and fast you will get a lower quality service. Fast-food is the perfect example. The system holds true for purchasing anything while travelling. I always choose cheap and quality, except in times where I am really limited on time. Normally you can make small tweaks to make this work for you. Ultimately you must make choices about what's most important to you.

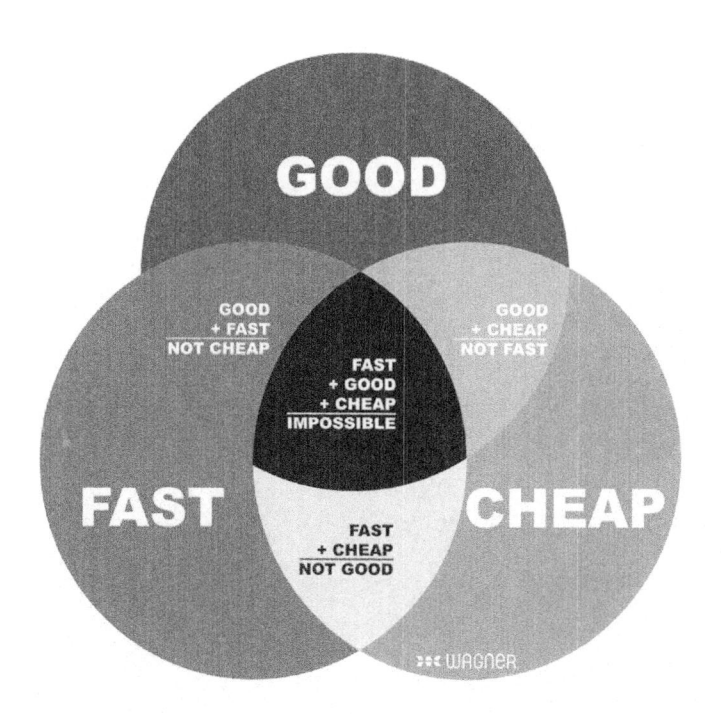

Our Writers

Phil Tang was born in London to immigrants, Phil graduated from The London School of Economics with a degree in Law. Now he travels full-time in search of travel bargains with his wife, dog and 1 year old daughter.

Ali Blythe has been writing about amazing places for 17 years. He loves travel and especially tiny budgets equalling big adventures nearly as much as his family. He recently trekked the Satopanth Glacier trekking through those ways from where no one else would trek. Ali is an adventurer by nature and bargainist by religion.

Michele Whitter writes about languages and travel. What separates her from other travel writers is her will to explain complex topics in a no-nonsense, straightforward way. She doesn't promise the world. But always delivers step-by-step methods you can immediately implement to travel on a budget.

Kim Mortimer, Kim's input on Super Cheap Insider Guides show you how to stretch your money further so you can travel cheaper, smarter, and with more wanderlust. She loves going over land on horses and helps us refine each guide to keep them effective.

Congratulations, you've saved money and done Good!

We donate 10% of all book profits to charity.

This year we are donating to Animal Shelters including one in Florence. The number of abandoned and homeless dogs and cats in Europe is over 100 million - the problem is particularly bad in the eastern and southern parts of Europe. I'm sure you've seen your fair share of abandoned dogs during your travels: its heart wrenching to see man's best friend starving and alone.

'My dog Gracie was abandoned on the highway in Slovakia. At just ten months old, they tied her to the railings and left her there. Animal Hope picked her up and took care of her and found her a home with us. She is now a healthy, happy girl and loves travelling with us, getting her nose into new smells and soliciting belly rubs from fellow travellers. What breaks my heart is her 'I haven't been abandoned dance'. She is always so happy that we haven't abandoned her when we collect her from outside a supermarket that she dances on her leash for several minutes. Watch her 'I haven't been abandoned dance' dance   . Money could never buy the happiness she has brought my family and me, but donations can help other abandoned animals like her to find loving homes.'

Katherine Huber, a contributor to Super Cheap Vienna.

Donations are made on the 4th January of each year on profits from the previous year. To nominate a charity to receive 10% of the proceeds of sales from our 2021 editions complete the form here: supercheapinsiderguides.com

Gracie

If you've found this book useful, please consider leaving a short review on Amazon. it would mean a lot.

Copyright

Published in Great Britain in 2019 by Super Cheap Insider Guides LTD.

Copyright © 2019 Super Cheap Insider Guides LTD.

The right of Phil G A Tang to be identified as the Author of the Work has been asserted in accordance with the Copyright, Designs and Patents Act 1988.

All rights reserved.

No part of this publication may be reproduced, stored in a retrieval system, or transmitted, in any form or by any means without the prior written permission of the publisher, nor be otherwise circulated in any form of binding or cover other than that in which it is published and without a similar condition being imposed on the subsequent purchaser.

All rights reserved. No part of this publication may be reproduced, distributed, or transmitted in any form or by any means, including photocopying, recording, or other electronic or mechanical methods, without the prior written permission of the publisher, except in the case of brief quotations embodied in critical reviews and certain other non-commercial uses permitted by copyright law.

HOW DID WE DO?

1 DID WE SAVE YOU MONEY?

2 DID YOU LEARN INSIDER INSIGHTS?

3 DID YOU GET A LIST OF THE BEST CHEAP EATS?

4 DID WE HELP YOU PLAN TO SAVE AND ENJOY MORE?

WHAT CAN WE DO BETTER?
EMAIL ME: PHILGTANG@GMAIL.COM

Where
NEXT?
ZURICH
2020 TRAVEL GUIDE
VENICE
2020 TRAVEL GUIDE
PRAGUE
2020 TRAVEL GUIDE
MILAN
2020 TRAVEL GUIDE
MARRAKESH
2020 TRAVEL GUIDE
AUSTIN
2020 TRAVEL GUIDE
CAPPADOCIA
2020 TRAVEL GUIDE
EDINBURGH
2020 TRAVEL GUIDE
ANTARCTICA
2020 TRAVEL GUIDE
SUPERCHEAPINSIDERGUIDES.COM

Printed in Great Britain
by Amazon